IMAGES
of America

EGG HARBOR CITY

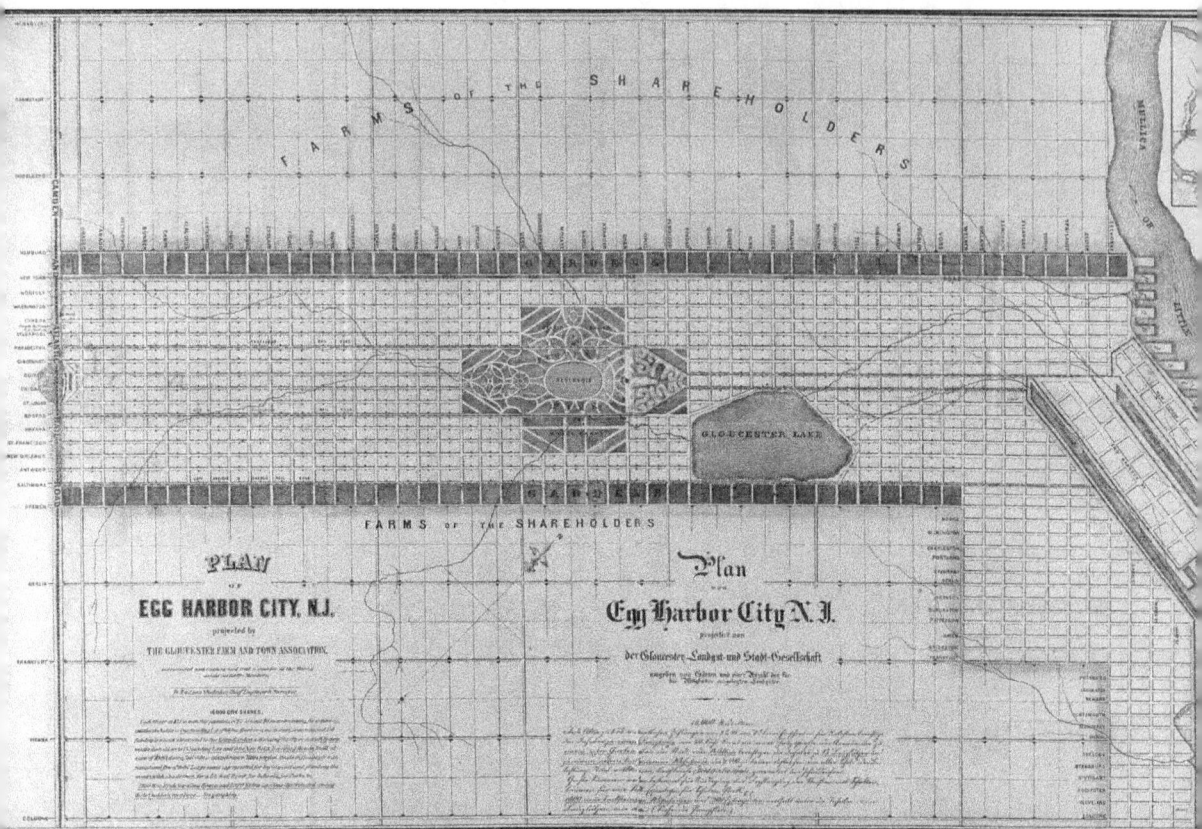

This 1850s map of Egg Harbor City was prepared for a sales brochure. The two dark rows are garden lots, with city lots between them and farm lots on the outside. The cross-shaped area contains a park, botanical gardens, and model farm next to the irregular-shaped Gloucester Lake. Four rail lines served the city residents and the harbor area at the right, each connecting with the Camden and Atlantic Railroad. (Roundhouse Museum.)

IMAGES
of America

EGG HARBOR CITY

Mark W. Maxwell

ARCADIA
PUBLISHING

Published by Arcadia Publishing
Charleston SC, Chicago IL, Portsmouth NH, San Francisco CA

Library of Congress Control Number: 2009925779

For all general information contact Arcadia Publishing at:
Telephone 843-853-2070
Fax 843-853-0044
E-mail sales@arcadiapublishing.com
For customer service and orders:
Toll-Free 1-888-313-2665

Visit us on the Internet at www.arcadiapublishing.com

Dedicated to the pioneers of Egg Harbor City, New Jersey

CONTENTS

Acknowledgments   6

Introduction   7

1.   Transportation   9

2.   Commerce   17

3.   Early Churches   53

4.   Music, Sports, and Organizations   63

5.   Public Services   89

6.   Sites and Landmarks   99

7.   The People   115

ACKNOWLEDGMENTS

Knowledge is symbolized by a lighted lamp. There are two types of acknowledgements to be addressed. The first is inspirational. Without inspiration, nothing would be ventured or gained. To that end, I wish to acknowledge four people whose guidance has inspired me to produce this photographic early history of Egg Harbor City.

The first two were sisters who built my lamp as Egg Harbor City schoolteachers. First was Anna R. Townsend, who taught second and then first grade for 44 years. One of her first students was her sister Norma, who would follow in her sister's footsteps as a fourth then third-grade teacher. After raising a son and daughter, she became a provisional teacher while completing her wartime-interrupted course of study, retiring after 26 years. Fourth grade is the year children are introduced to New Jersey history, but thanks to Aunt Anna and my mother, history was always present in my life. All those family trips we took had a historical lesson to be learned.

My third inspiration was Adele Baden, who knew where everything was in Egg Harbor City's Roundhouse Museum. With her help as museum curator, I was able to apply my computer experience to local history. Now, after the passing of Adele, much is available with a few mouse clicks. Adele refueled my lamp.

The fourth person is Erin Rocha, who lit the flame of my lamp that started this book.

The second type is the people who helped me prepare this book. The main sources of information are the manuscripts of Antoinette Doell, teacher, principal, and historian of early Egg Harbor City; Dr. Dieter Cunz's manuscript, *Egg Harbor City: New Germany in New Jersey*; and city historian Ron Hesse. Additional help came from historical society members (my wife Patricia, Richard Colby, Geraldine Fenstermaker, Ruth Ellen Gronlund, Hazel Zimmer Mueller, Dennis Nicelor, and Roy Weiler to name but a few), the churches and organizations (F&AM, EHCFD, and EHCPD) who opened their archives, and the many residents who provided additional photographs and information. A special thanks to Walter Ellis of Aero Club of Pennsylvania for identification of the Wright Flyer on page 12.

Unless otherwise noted, photographs are from the Roundhouse Museum Collection.

INTRODUCTION

About 20 miles northwest of Atlantic City on US-30 lies the small community of Egg Harbor City. Once known as the most German city in the United States, it is now a somewhat typical semirural melting pot of many cultures and races.

Originally founded as an escape from the large cites of their adopted land, the German settlers found this area a place of cultural solidatiry. They assembled a group of prominent people to create a habitat within the wilderness of southern New Jersey, where only sand, weeds, and mosquitoes were found in abundance. On December 14, 1854, the Gloucester Farm and Town Association (GFTA) was chartered to purchase more than 38,000 acres of land from the powerful iron-producing Richards and Colwell families. The city was originally envisioned in two parts, with the western part centered at Cedar Bridge and the second part several miles east at Gloucester Landing. Within a few months, the duality was rejected and development centered near the railroad.

Engineers produced a workable plan that included blocks of four major types of land classifications: city lots, garden lots, farm lots, and wharf lots. The blocks were crisscrossed by parallel 70-foot-wide avenues and 48-foot-wide streets. Every fifth avenue was widened, three of them to 100 feet and one to 200 feet. Every seventh street served as a 60-foot-wide artery from the city into the surrounding farms, providing access to the market area. Between the avenues ran 30-foot-wide back streets designed to provide the utilities of the future and a second street access to each city lot. All of the avenues were named for important ports of the time; the back streets became numbered "terraces," and with the exception of Atlantic Street along the Camden and Atlantic Railroad (C&A Railroad) right-of-way, the streets were alphabetically named for people who played an important part in German life and society. In addition, the four extra-wide avenues were to have rail lines run down their centers, from the C&A Railroad to the Mullica River. The two interior lines were for passenger movement, the eastern line was for freight from the harbor area to the C&A Railroad railhead, and the western line was part of the proposed New York and Norfolk Air Line Railroad.

With the infrastructure planned, the general appearance of the city came next. Near the center of the plan would be a large park area with a reservoir at the confluence of three creeks that then flowed into Gloucester Lake. Around this man-made lake, engineers planned botanical gardens, a model farm, and parks. In addition, two parks (Turner and Sänger) were placed at the western and eastern entrances by the railroad. A three-block "Marktplatz" was planned on the C&A Railroad at the middle of the city with a great passenger terminal on the opposite side of the tracks. Within the marketplace would be Excursion Hall, to be used for meetings of all types and a school. The streets were to be curbed and lined with shade trees. The design called for two kinds of city blocks, containing either thirty-two 40 by 150-foot lots or 16 double-wide lots. Garden lots at the edges of the city were 40 feet wide and 330 feet deep—there were no "terraces" here. The farm lots were slated to be 5 and 20 acres each, while the wharf lots remained undefined.

When it came to populating "the great German experiment," promoters used many different approaches. Advertisements were placed in German newspapers across the United States and Germany, the latter causing diplomatic problems. GFTA divided the city into 16,000 city shares, offered at $75/share, each of which entitled the owner to one 40 by 150-foot building lot and one garden lot at the edge of the city. A more prosperous investor could purchase 14 shares, which entitled the owner to 15 building lots and one new brick dwelling house, at the cost of $400. Both purchases required an initial subscription fee of $3 in addition to a $2.50 monthly payment per lot. The directors of the C&A Railroad also made inducements to build near their tracks. Anyone who built a $300 house within two blocks of the railroad was offered six months of free travel on the railroad plus an additional six months of half-fare travel. The goal of this was to produce an impressive sight of large homes within view of the railroad station at Liverpool Avenue.

Commercial growth started with small, individual businesses: cobblers, dressmakers, and tailors, butchers and bakers, candy-makers, harness-makers, and wagon-builders. Coopers were kept busy making the barrels for all the wine and beer being produced. Soon, industrial growth began with large vineyards, breweries, porcelain plants, brickworks, tailoring shops, and glassworks. Numerous hotels and boardinghouses sprang up to house the rapidly swelling population.

Everything progressed even better than the town's founders had originally envisioned—until Fort Sumter. As the Civil War exploded onto the scene, many men left their homes and families to enlist in the German regiments being formed in Philadelphia. The GFTA struggled to collect taxes from shareholders not living in the settlement, and the reduced revenues limited what public improvements could be made. The planned dredging of the river was halted, allowing only shallow-draught boats access to the few docks along the river. By 1865, the vast wartime expansion of rail networks had rendered Egg Harbor commercially nonviable. Despite all this, as its soldiers returned, the city continued to expand and prosper.

This photographic folio of Egg Harbor City will give you an idea of what it was like to grow up here in the wilderness of southern New Jersey as residents struggled to maintain their sense of German pride. Many of the old family names remain in town, though some have changed spelling or pronunciation to be "more American"—including our most famous name, which, as fate would have it, is not German at all. When Louis N. Renault came from France to the United States in the early 1860s, he noticed that Americans pronounced the last letters in his name, making it "REN–ALLT" rather than "RAY–NO," and that is the way it has remained. The end of the Civil War brought new ethnic groups to man the fields, build the factories, and expand the railroads. English, Irish, Italians, and former slaves came here for a new start in life. Although the city is now multicultural, in a few churches every Christmas, you can still hear "Silent Night" sung in German.

One

TRANSPORTATION

Transportation was the key to the founding of Egg Harbor City. Before the 1850s, people and produce moved by foot or boat along the rivers and coastlines. Few settlements in Atlantic County in 1838 were inaccessible by navigable waterways. One was Gloucester Landing near the Mullica River.

The Camden and Atlantic Railroad (C&A Railroad) provided the first excursion to Atlantic City, passing a few miles below Gloucester Landing. On that first trip in July 1854 were several German Philadelphia businessmen viewing the long stretches of lightly forested land during refueling and watering at Cedar Bridge. They felt they found an ideal site for their people to settle and establish a German community away from the harassing nativistic Know-Nothings.

These businessmen formed the Gloucester Farm and Town Association, bought 30,000 acres from the Colwell and Ford families, and laid out an orderly city street plan from the railroad to the Mullica River. A central city evolved with commercial and industrial sites surrounded by agricultural areas. Initially, a harbor dock at Gloucester Landing handled coastal schooners and plans were afoot to dredge the river, but these simply became more casualties of the Civil War. The only reminders of the planned shipping center are the Seal of the City that shows a square-rigged sailing ship on a river, the annual election of a harbormaster, and the age-old question that Egg Harbor citizens grow up hearing: "Where is the harbor?"

The C&A Railroad played an increasing role in the city's development. During the Centennial Celebration of 1876, Egg Harbor City's wines had made a big splash in the competitions there and later in the 1878 Paris Wine Exhibition. The railroad offered a wine-tasting excursion to wine merchants of New York City and Philadelphia to show off the wines and more than 800 acres of grape vineyards.

In the ensuing years would come county, state, and national highways, several railroads, public service buses (now New Jersey Transit), and the nearby Atlantic City Airport.

The railroad brought more than freight and regular passengers to Egg Harbor City. In 1912, Bull Moose presidential candidate Theodore Roosevelt stopped at the Liverpool Avenue crossing of the Pennsylvania Railroad. As this photograph affirms, Roosevelt drew an enthusiastic crowd of all ages, and he received rousing cheers by starting his speech "My fellow Dutchmen of Egg Harbor City."

Reading-Seashore Railroad engine No. 348 pulls into the Egg Harbor City Station on its way to Atlantic City. This railroad used similar camelback locomotives on narrow-gauge tracks in competition with the Pennsylvania Railroad that paralleled its right-of-way from Camden to Atlantic City. They later merged into the Pennsylvania-Reading Seashore Line and abandoned the narrow-gauge line.

10

This 2-6-0 F3c Baldwin Locomotive (work No. 19018), built in 1901, was bought new by the West Jersey and Seashore Railroad (WJ&S Railroad). Its 62-inch drivers were driven by two 20-by-28-inch cylinders to move the 165,900-pound engine down the tracks. The WJ&S Railroad later merged into the Pennsylvania Railroad. This photograph was taken at Liverpool Avenue looking toward the old C&A Railroad station. (Author's collection.)

This photograph shows one of the several steam engines used by the early Pennsylvania Railroad on its line from Philadelphia to Atlantic City. This engine is a Baldwin Type B No. 857, a 4-4-0 manufactured in 1890. It sits on the main rails of the line in front of Henry Kuehnle's hotel at Liverpool Avenue and Atlantic Street.

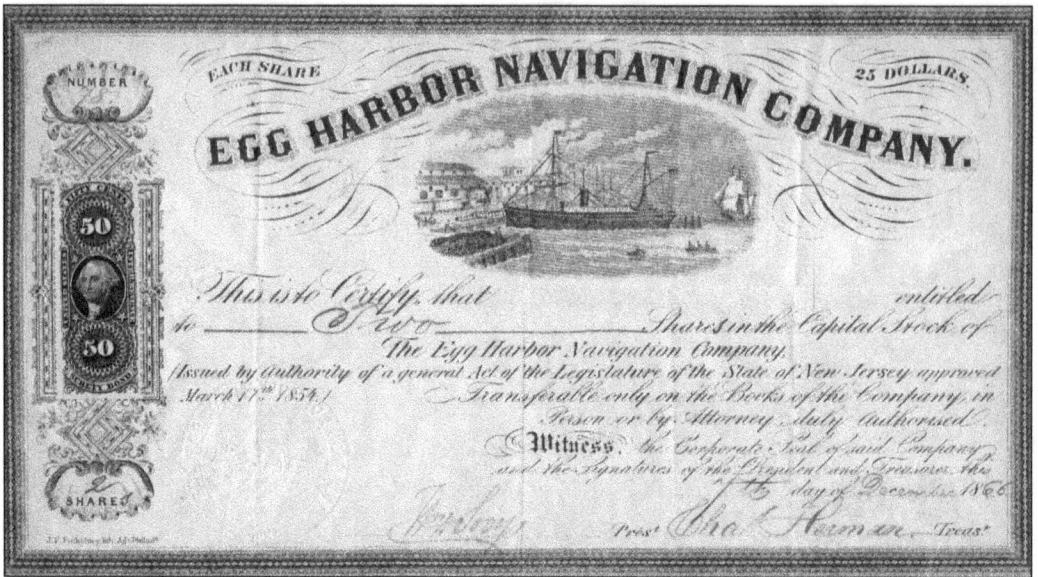

This stock certificate, dated 1866, shows that plans for developing the harbor were still proceeding immediately after the Civil War. The drawing on the certificate illustrates how Gloucester Landing was to appear, with its wharves and trains connected to the C&A Railroad. The schooner *Eureka* made trips to Gloucester Landing from major East Coast ports until the early 1870s.

This Wright Flyer Model B, towed behind an automobile, made an uncommon visitor to the city in 1912. Marshall Earl Reid of Philadelphia received pilot license No. 114, and in 1912, with his mechanic Orton Hoover, he carried 15,645 pieces of mail in a seven flight post office test program from Ocean City to Stone Harbor—the longest such flight to that time.

These c. 1928 postcards show the automotive transportation hub of Egg Harbor City looking northwest along the White Horse Pike. The pike is not running one way, although the motorists make it looks that way. The single three-colored traffic signal is just to the right and midway up the nearest pole. Across the intersection are the American Store and the city firehouse to the right. The view below is looking southeast toward Lincoln Park in the background. On the left is Dr. Boysen's drugstore, and Max Rittenberg's Dry Goods store is on the right. White Horse Pike became US-30, connecting Philadelphia and Atlantic City with regularly scheduled buses such as the Quaker State Lines coach seen here and marked traffic lanes. (Both, Ron Hesse collection.)

This picture shows the Egg Harbor City Pennsylvania Railroad passenger station on the south side of the tracks (actually in Galloway Township) at Philadelphia Avenue about 1905. The station also housed the office of the South Jersey Express Company (owners of the horse and wagon seen here) on the left end of the building.

This picture shows Egg Harbor City's Reading Railroad station (also in Galloway Township) near Aloe Street and Philadelphia Avenue, the present location of the Senn Oil Company. It had more space than the Pennsylvania Railroad station, which allowed for the planting of gardens and the construction of a large parking area for automobiles and wagons.

Agassiz Street (today's White Horse Pike) was the main connecting east-west road between the communities of Hammonton and Absecon. Seen here around 1900, it is a packed gravel road serving both horse-drawn wagons and automobiles. The nearby house is on New York Avenue, and further down the road stands Garnich's Hotel at Hamburg Avenue. The distant approaching automobile is crossing Cedar Creek, not far from the starting place of Egg Harbor City.

This 1904 photograph shows Oswald Bott with his wife and their daughter Elsie preparing for a ride in their Curved Dash Oldsmobile. (The age of the automobile is difficult to determine because of its many additions and the fact that the Curved Dash Oldsmobile's 1901 through 1907 models were exactly alike.) Bott owned Bott's Hardware store, located at 213 Philadelphia Avenue.

These pictures show a group of motorcyclists in front of Van's Café at 113 Philadelphia Avenue. The window in the extreme left of the upper image is possibly that of a florist's shop; it contains several potted plants and the word "plants" on the glass. To the right of Van's is the Egg Harbor Hotel, located at 115 Philadelphia Avenue. The keystone sign by the door indicates the presence of a local pay telephone station. From left, the first three and the sixth motorcycles are 1910 Harley Davidsons, while the fourth and fifth are 1911 Indians. In the photograph above, the men on their cycles are, from left to right, Henry Goetz, William Senn, William Deppi, Sal Zito, Jake Kutz sitting behind John Husta, and Bob Leseman. Standing next to William Senn with his arms crossed is Adolph Joseph. Helping to place the date about June 1912 are the two styles of 48-star flags, settled by President Taft's order on June 24.

Two

COMMERCE

The Fortbildung Verein (Founder's Association) counted on the German people to persevere. The early settlers found an abundant water supply for industry and agriculture; soil suitable for growing wine grapes; large stands of Eastern White Cedar amongst pines and oaks that attracted sawyers and builders; clay deposits for bricks, clay pipes, and porcelain; and white sand for making glass.

The city produced many fine wines and beer. That meant work for coopers, blacksmiths, and wagon-makers. Good wine and beer needed good cigars, made by the city's 23 cigar-makers.

The automobile and train brought a hotel industry. Many lodgings were built between the railroad and Agassiz Street. As years passed, automobiles and trucks replaced the horses and wagons. The C&A Railroad merged into the Pennsylvania Railroad, and the Reading Railroad soon followed. Large grocery companies (Acme and A&P) competed with the mom-and-pop stores.

In 1884, a Building and Loan Association provided capital for building homes, stores, and factories; the Egg Harbor City Commercial Bank opened in 1888. Thirty years later, World War I brought a clothing industry that employed nearly 50 percent of the city. World War II drove the clothing industry to new heights, and local boatbuilding was revitalized. Small boats had been built here for years, but now the war demanded larger craft, so C. P. Leek and Son began making 80-foot submarine chasers. After the war, their newfound experience helped them build 65-foot pleasure cruisers.

To keep the community informed, the first newspaper, *Der Pilot*, was founded in 1858, followed by others like *Der Zeitgeist, Deutscher Herald*, and the *Egg Harbor Tribune*. In 1900, *The News* was the city's first all-English newspaper. An electricity generation plant came in 1898. The water plant was built in 1896, and in 1903, the Enterprise Gas Company began to produce quality gas for homes and industry. The city's first telephone company came in 1904.

Other Egg Harbor factories included Samuel Winterbottom's "bone mill," which manufactured bone-handled knives; the Liberty Cut Glass Company, which created highly facetted glassware; the Nurre Mirror Company (which replaced Liberty after a devastating fire); and the Bloch Go-Cart Company, which produced reed furniture, invalid chairs, go-carts, and the famous Atlantic City Boardwalk rolling chairs.

Der Egg Harbor Pilot.

Unabhängiges Organ
für die
Mitglieder und Freunde der Gloucester Landgut- und Stadtgesellschaft, mit den Tendenzen des Conservativen Männervereins.
"Im Gedeihen des Ganzen liegt das Wohl des Einzelnen."
Herausgegeben von Franz Scheu.

Dritter Jahrgang.   Egg Harbor City, den 7. Dezember 1861   Nummer 35

Der Zeitgeist.

Motto: Entschieden aber besonnen Vorwärts.

M. Stutzbach & Co. Herausgeber.

Jahrgang 10.   Egg Harbor City, N. J., Sonnabend, den 25. März 1876.   Nummer 1.

The Spirit of the Times.

A Weekly German News Paper devoted to the principles of Humanity, Education Interstate and General Improvement.

ATLANTIC JOURNAL.

ONE COPY, ONE YEAR, $2.00.   **M. STUTZBACH & SONS**, Publishers.   ONE COPY, SIX MONTHS, $1.00.

VOL. VI.   EGG HARBOR CITY, N. J., THURSDAY, AUGUST 17, 1876.   NO. 19.

Carneval-Zeitung.

Ein Organ für Förderung höheren Blödsinns junger und alter Narren.

Herausgegeben von Elias Vorwärts. — Verantwortlicher Redakteur Hans Keinerda.

99. Jahrgang.   Egg Harbor City im Narrenmonat 1879.   Nro. 00.

EVERYBODY READS   # THE NEWS   Egg Harbor's Leading Paper

ISSUED EVERY WEDNESDAY   Reliable News That's Fit to Print   PUBLISHED BY CHARLES M. BREDER   PRICE 3 CENTS A COPY

NUMBER 71   EGG HARBOR CITY N. J., THURSDAY, JULY 12, 1917   VOLUME 12

Egg Harbor Pilot - Tribune

VOL 67.   EGG HARBOR CITY, N. J., FRIDAY, DECEMBER 18, 1925   No. 16

Commerce depends upon the ability to advertise; throughout the late 19th and early 20th centuries, merchants and manufacturers found the most effective real estate for advertising in the pages of local newspapers. Above are the banners of just six of the newspapers founded in Egg Harbor City. The oldest, *Der Pilot,* was founded in 1858 and edited by Hugo Maas for 27 years until bought by Charles Kroekel in 1904. *Der Zeitgeist* was founded by Moritz Stutzbach in March 1866. It was sold to George Breder who renamed it *Deutscher Herald.* When George became postmaster in 1898, he sold his business to his brother Frank. About 1899, George W. Otto offered aid and support to start an English-language newspaper to Frank Breder. He edited *The News* until 1903 when Frank took over. *Carneval-Zeitung* was the joke paper of Lenten carnival times; its byline trumpeted it as "[A]n organ for the challenge of prominent nonsense of young and old fools." The *Egg Harbor Pilot-Tribune* resulted from the merger of the *Tribune* and *Der Pilot.*

This photograph shows the office and staff of *The News* in front of the building at 129 Cincinnati Avenue. The typesetting and linotype machines were in the small addition to the rear of the building. The house on the left was later owned by George Gries, the last editor and publisher of the paper.

The intersection of Cincinnati Avenue and Agassiz Street shows some of the typical houses of about 1905. Since it was a major intersection, this corner was selected to receive the single street light, seen at top center. The low building at the right was the print shop that produced the *Egg Harbor Pilot* newspaper.

Of Louis N. Renault's once-proud Columbia Vineyard house and buildings seen here on the northwest side of Philadelphia Avenue beyond Fichte Street, only the house remains—the cleared fields have reverted to forest. Today the city's revitalization project is building some 20 large houses on the grounds.

One of the city's most successful businesses is the House of Renault. This photograph shows the bottling plant and Renault bottle sign at Norfolk Avenue and the White Horse Pike. Renault did most of its bottling here in the middle years, in the former Hammonton Shoe Factory. It had a pipeline to a railroad siding for unloading tank-cars of grape juice from its California vineyards directly into steel tanks.

The above early-1900s photograph shows many of the pieces of equipment used by Renault in bottling their wines, many of which can be seen today in the winery's museum. It is believed that the man at the rear in suspenders in Louis Renault's son Felix. The lower photograph resembles the one above, but it shows the bottling of American champagne in another Renault cellar. Because of the gas pressure within the bottles, metal caps and twisted wire kept the corks in place, as seen in the boxes on the floor. These were then covered with a metal foil. (Renault Winery.)

WINE VAULTS OF
JOHN. H. BANNIHR. EGG HARBOR. CITY. NEW. JERSEY.
CAPACITY 50, 000 GALLONS.

Above is the first-stage building of John Bannihr's winery on Liverpool Avenue. The photograph looks north from across Fifth Terrace, showing the various entrance levels to the building and Bannihr's use of local stone in its construction. Bannihr wines won medals in Philadelphia in 1879 and at the 1893 Columbian Exposition in Chicago. The photograph below shows the winery after its purchase by Hiram T. Dewey and shows the third-stage building with the stone addition to the terrace side of the structure. Various doors are clearly seen here, along with several barrels marked Dewey by the two original loading doors. Above the winery's roof is the top floor of the American Hotel, and left of center is the tower of Kopf's Hotel with its small band stage.

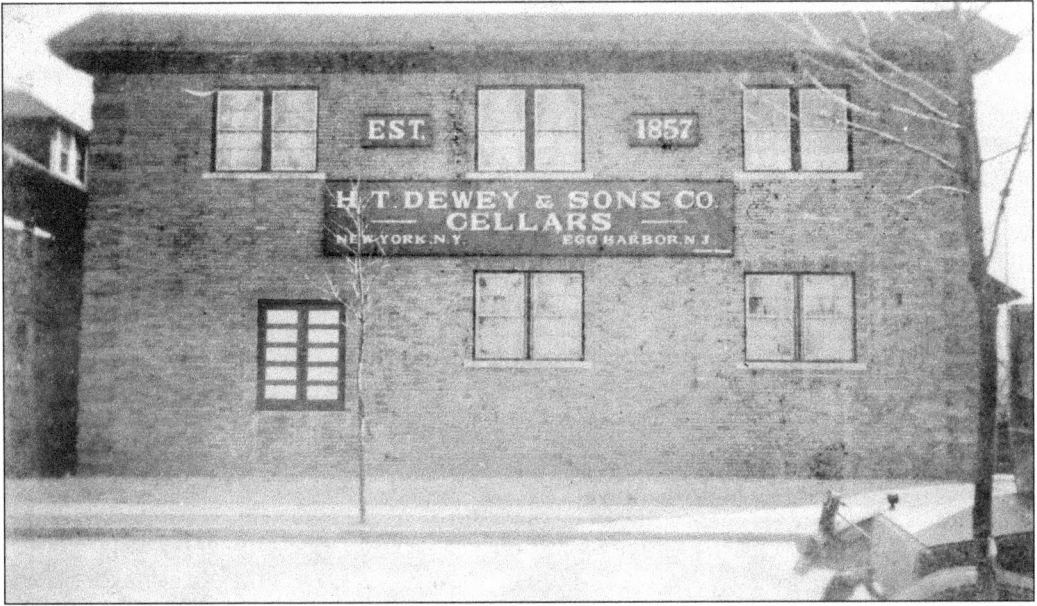

This is the office addition with a loading dock made by H. T. Dewey and Sons to the original Bannihr Winery on Liverpool Avenue. Hiram Dewey came to Egg Harbor City from New York City in 1881 and remained here. Dewey was a long-standing member of the Free and Accepted Masons, and the local Masonic Lodge is named in his honor.

Among the Roundhouse Museum Collection are these two medals awarded to the John Bannihr Winery. Bannihr received the silver medal for his 1879 exhibit of still wines in Philadelphia, and the bronze medal on the right for his exhibit at the 1893 Columbian Exposition in Chicago. Soon after this, Hiram T. Dewey purchased the winery.

John Schuster Sr. is seen amongst the grapes in his vineyard at 502 St. Louis Avenue. One of the premier wine producers of the city, Schuster's family continued to provide wines from its cellars until the 1970s, when John Schuster III ceased production of his carefully prepared sacramental wine. Bottles of their wines continue to be found in old cellars today.

Egg Harbor citizens celebrate the end of Prohibition—Repeal Day—in December 1933 with a barrel of Renault's best on Philadelphia Avenue. Many people have turned out to get their first legal sample of alcohol since January 1920. Helping to pour the wine near the barrel and in front of the accordion player is 25-year-old Mildred Norman (who, 20 years later, would become "Peace Pilgrim") and Renault employee Henry "Sparky" Fikes (wearing a white apron). (Renault Winery.)

The Egg Harbor Brick Company was located between Darmstadt and Heidelberg Avenues on County Road west of the city limits, opposite the Butterhof Feed Store on the White Horse Pike. A railroad spur crossed the roadway to bring coal for the kilns and take out the finished bricks, but it was removed about 1928 when the White Horse Pike was widened. Thus isolated, the brickworks soon closed.

This c. 1900 photograph shows Henry Kann's lumberyard south of the Pennsylvania-Seashore Line (P-SL) tracks and Philadelphia Avenue. The yard offered lumber, millwork, and coal in competition with Egg Harbor Coal and Lumber just across the tracks. Behind the buildings are double-sided signs facing P-SL and the Reading Railroad.

25

George and William Senn Sr. owned the Senn Brothers plumbing supply company (above), which occupied the center two buildings in the 200 block of Philadelphia Avenue and the shop building on Sixth Terrace (located behind the house to the right of the storefront). In the photograph below, standing from left to right in front of the shop building are Louis "Chick" Lauer (holding clamps), Edward Senn (with moustache), George Senn, two unidentified, Adolph Joseph (seated), John Tyler (the Senns' brother-in-law), and William Senn Sr. (behind the motorcycle). The shop picture below was taken before 1911, when the right house in the picture above was built. Across Philadelphia Avenue one can see the Obergfell dry goods store. Today the wooden houses have been replaced by brick ones containing the plumbing supply business (now operated by George Senn's great-grandson) and an upstairs apartment.

AURORA HOTEL

Egg Harbor City, N. J.

Originally Ertell's Hotel, the Aurora Hotel owned by Frederick Lott served numerous purposes on Liverpool Avenue for many years. The Aurora had meeting rooms, a billiard parlor, bowling alley, and even an indoor rifle range. A large ballroom provided a venue for theatrical stage and musical shows, hosted balls, and was the site of many school and semiprofessional basketball games. It also served as a meeting hall for the American Organization of Automobilists.

This photograph shows that the Aurora Hotel was more than a local business and entertainment facility; it was also used by county and state organizations. This 1915 view of Liverpool Avenue shows part of a parade for a Shrine convention. Of note in the upper right corner is the sign for the electric charging station, used for the electric automobiles of that period.

Aurora Hotel was one of Egg Harbor City's finer eating establishments in the early 1900s. This photograph shows one of the smaller dining rooms used by various organizations for their meetings. Pictured from left to right are (seated) Frederick Bergman, Frederick Schwenger, unidentified, Harry Rupp, Henry Fisher, George Karrer, John Lehneis, and George Mueller; (standing) Henry Kahn and an unidentified man.

The American Hotel, like the Aurora Hotel, was a focal point for travelers through Egg Harbor City. As seen in this 1905 photograph, the dusty dirt highways of the time created a lot of thirsty motorcyclists, who would come to the hotel, the Golden Ox tavern, and the neighboring Columbia House for local beer and food.

This is the Continental Hotel located at 137–139 Philadelphia Avenue. Jacob Daetwiler purchased the hotel in 1884 and is believed to be the man standing by the main door. He sold the hotel to Charles Hall in 1897, who in turn sold it to Jacob Ruetsch. In the photograph below, taken about 1900, Ruetsch has raised a porch in front of the brick building next door that is also signed as part of the hotel. This section contained a pool hall, cigar store, and liquor store on the main floor while a Rathskeller entrance was made below the high hotel porch on the left. The wooden building was razed more than 60 years ago. The brick building is to be razed following a devastating fire in 2008.

William Oeser's Central Hotel stood at the corner of Buffalo Avenue and Arago Street. A popular eatery, it offered oysters and—as the paper sign in the window advertises—sauerkraut lunches. A public Delaware and Atlantic long distance telephone was also available. The Central would later become an apartment house.

This is a picture of the Golden Hotel at 121–123 Philadelphia Avenue, bought by John Reichenbach in 1904. He also had a tobacco shop on the left side of the building. John and his wife, Louisa, ran these businesses until 1909. (Ethel Meincke Roesch.)

Bissig's Hotel was one of many on Philadelphia Avenue. It was located on the northwest corner at Arago Street, which today is occupied by the Wachovia Bank. The large building on the right was a millinery shop and the home of the Arnold family. Between the two was the General Stahel Post No. 62 of the Grand Army of the Republic.

Egg Harbor City was on the rise when the Civil War started in 1861. Although many of the streets still had tree stumps in them, their commercial and social interests were going strong. Seen here is evidence that the Egg Harbor Bank was strong enough to issue its own demand currency in 1861.

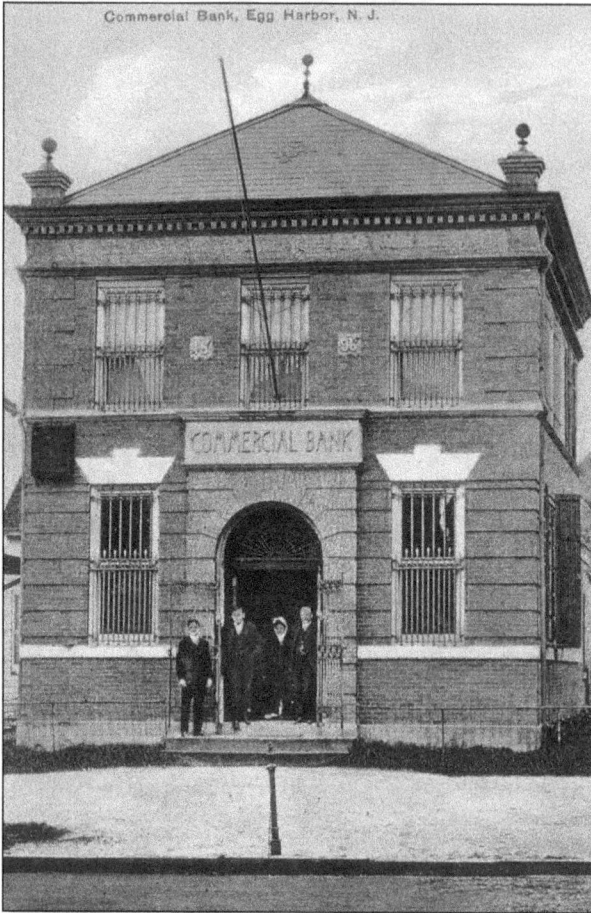

Commercial Bank, Egg Harbor, N. J.

COMMERCIAL BANK

The 1908 photographic postcard at left shows the Egg Harbor City Commercial Bank (EHCCB) at 134 Philadelphia Avenue. The date blocks between the second-floor windows indicate a construction date of 1896. The black box on the left of the building is the bell box for the electric vault alarm system, the first of its kind on the mainland. The electric chimes of the bank clock rang on the quarter hours. Later the EHCCB added an entrance with granite steps and two granite columns, and about 1922, this entrance was enlarged by jacking up the building and moving it back some 20 feet from the steps. A new section was then constructed between the steps and the original building. In the photograph of the transformed building below, only the roof of the original structure is visible.

Egg Harbor City supported several bakeries. The one owned by Anton Weisbecker at the corner of Philadelphia Avenue and Arago Street used high-temperature steam to do its baking. In 1910, one could ask for telephone number 12-05, order a cake and ice cream, and have it delivered in this truck.

This photograph shows a delivery truck owned by the Christian Atz Brewery, which operated from 1888 until it was closed in 1920 at the start of Prohibition. The brewery's cedar-water beer was well liked in the area and kept this truck running from here to places between Atlantic City and Hammonton. Atz Brewery was one of the first in the nation to use bottles for their beer.

Above, a decorated car drives past the Colonial Theater and Golden Eagle Hall on the left. The Golden Eagle Hall building served as Antioch Commandery of Castle 44 of the Knights of the Golden Eagle. The sign above the door to the second floor reads "Egg Harbor City Telephone Company." Today, after considerable remodeling, this building is the Hiram T. Dewey Masonic Lodge. The theater, shown below in 1921, was built by Emil Weiler in 1914 and opened with vaudeville and silent pictures. The building also contained the City Clerk's Office on the right. It was a center of entertainment until the early 1960s when local drive-in movies and larger multiscreen theaters closed its doors for good.

One of the largest clothing manufacturers in Egg Harbor City was the Theodore Baulig Underwear factory. Originally from Baltimore, Baulig erected this building in 1906 on Buffalo Avenue across from Lincoln Park and next to Liberty Cut Glass Company. When Baulig returned to Baltimore in 1932, the Commercial Bank took over the building. It was demolished in the 1950s. Recently, Baulig's house was demolished to build a Select Bank.

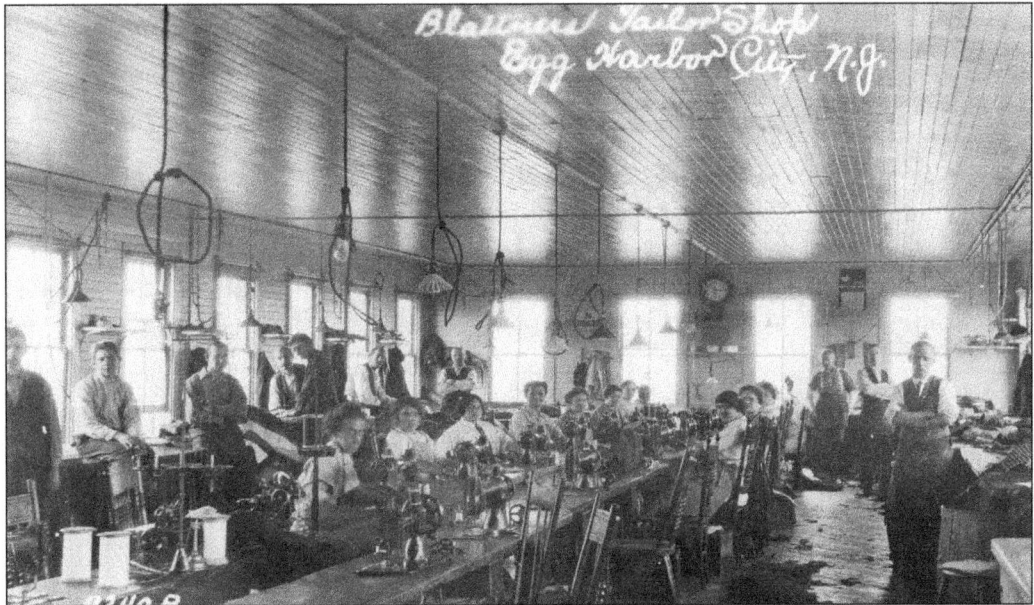

This is a September 1914 view of the Charles Blattner Tailor Shop located at 344 Eighth Terrace. The men did all the cutting while the women did the sewing. During this time, almost 50 percent of the city's population was involved in the garment industry, which included 10 major shops and many more individual and specialty shops.

The Enterprise Gas Company was founded in 1903 to produce gas for factories and homes to use in lighting, cooking, and heating. The company production facilities were located at the south end of Lincoln Park across the street from Liberty Cut Glass. Among the founders were Samuel Winterbottom, Henry Kuehnle, George Mueller, and Frederick Schuhardt. Dismantled in 1959, the site caused groundwater pollution that was not cleaned up until the 1990s.

This photograph shows the Sinclair gasoline station at Liverpool Avenue and the White Horse Pike about 1940. The building was purchased by W. Haines Maxwell after World War II and for many years housed the Egg Harbor City Police Volunteer Ambulance Squad. To the left can be seen the Dewey Winery building and the Baulig house behind it. Today the building houses Wimberg Funeral Home vehicles.

Walter Henschel is seen here fueling a customer's car in front of his Tydol gas station at Washington Avenue and the White Horse Pike in the early 1930s. The building later became a Sunoco station run by Henschel, his son-in-law Robert Peterson, and now his grandchildren as an independent repair shop. Behind the garage is the kiln building that belonged to Walter's father-in-law, Edmund Einsiedel, the last potter in the city.

Here Edmund Einsiedel stands with his dog in his general store located on the southwest corner of Third Terrace and County Road. Some of the items here are familiar today, such as Cracker Jacks, Saltine Crackers, and Rold Gold pretzels. Einsiedel also sold pottery from his kiln, including terra-cotta flower pots and fern-like edging for gardens and cemetery lots.

The American Stores Company occupied several locations, this one being the northwest corner of Philadelphia Avenue and the White Horse Pike. Competition was fierce with family stores on each corner and the A&P just 60 feet away. The 1928 prices shown here include bread at 8¢ a loaf and coffee at 39¢ a pound. The interior of the American Store, below, was typical for 1923, with a deli showing its open-air hanging meats and cheeses on one side of the store, and canned and boxed goods on the other, like Puffed Wheat, chocolate cake, and a 1-pound can of Asco salmon for 21¢ per can. From left to right are butcher Harvey Schneck, unidentified, cashier Julia Karrer, store manager Theodore Ficken Sr., clerk Henry Morgenweck, and assistant store manager Clarence "Bricky" Jones.

This was the packinghouse of William Zuefle and Company, manufacturer of Atlantic Brand Food Products, which also included fruits and vegetables. It was located near the northwest corner of Cincinnati Avenue and Beethoven Street. It once belonged to Harry May. On the left are the Odd Fellows Lodge on Philadelphia Avenue and a house on Sixth Terrace. Both of these latter structures remain today.

Gertrude Arnoldt took this 1925 photograph of the house at 119 Philadelphia Avenue and the Arnoldt Meat Market next door. Standing in the center is August Arnoldt, owner of both the market and the house. Sitting on the porch rail is his daughter Ethel, who later married Carl Weiler. In 1940, Carl turned the front of the first floor of the house into his barbershop. (Roy Weiler.)

This photograph was taken looking southeast at the Robert Ohnmeiss hardware store on the corner of Cincinnati Avenue and Arago Street following a heavy 1908 snowstorm. Today the building has been remodeled and functions as an apartment house.

The clothing factory of Shindel and Stern was built on the eastern side of Philadelphia Avenue near Atlantic Street about 1920. Shindel and Stern ran a modern, well-ventilated block factory building and took pride in hiring many black workers as well as white workers. When the industry wound down, the factory was abandoned and eventually torn down.

The *c.* 1890 photograph above shows Charles G. Dihlmann's store on the corner of Chicago Avenue and Arago Street. Charles is believed to be the man standing on the right. Charles had worked as a grocery clerk in his father's store, taking over when his father died. When Charles himself died, his son-in-law, John Heniss, ran the store under his own name while Mrs. Dihlmann retained ownership of the property. The building later became Walter Grawe's tailor shop. In the photograph below, notice the addition of an oil streetlamp and electrical wires above the store sign that help establish this as the more recent of the two photographs. Later, when John Heniss operated the store, an electric streetlamp had taken the gas lamp's place. Today the building is a private home, and the porch seen here has been enclosed.

The Liberty Cut Glass factory was founded in 1902 and located at the corner of Buffalo Avenue and Atlantic Street. All cutting took place in the wooden building. The flat-roofed brick building housed the offices of Liberty Cut Glass, and the hip-roofed brick structure is the Baulig and Company underwear factory with its water tank above the roof. Initially cutting imported glass blanks, Liberty eventually built its own furnace, allowing the company to produce several different colored glasses. These were used to produce some very collectible Depression Glass pieces, and later enamels and gold trim were added. Furnaces also caused several fires, when molten glass poured onto the wooden floors. One of these fires destroyed the cutting building and its equipment. The photograph below shows the office staff in front of the office building facing Lincoln Park on Buffalo Avenue.

This view of the cutting room floor at Liberty Cut Glass shows an unidentified worker holding a large vase that is priced at $4. Work stations lined the outside walls; a central shaft of pulleys supplied power to the wheels with large leather belts. With few lights, empty sockets, unshielded belts and pulleys, and no masks to protect workers from the silica and lead dust, the factory shown here would be an OSHA nightmare today. Below is a copy of a 1918 advertisement found in the school newspaper *Echo*, showing the array of items the factory produced. The most expensive item was the water set, on sale at $8, which today could easily cost one hundred times that price.

Special Sale.

The Items Illustrated are Unsurpassed.

No. 1, Fern Dish	$3 00	No. 11, Sug. and Cream	$2 25
2, Vase, 9½"	1 00	12, Compote	1 00
3, " 6"	1 00	13, Bowl, 8"	3 00
4, " 12"	4 00	14, " 7"	2 00
5, Water Set	8 00	15, Deep Nappy, 6"	1 25
6, Mar. Set	1 00	16, Vase, 12"	4 50
7, Compote	2 25	17, May Set	1 00
8, Cr. & Cheese	1 50	18, Celery	3 00
9, Sug. & Cream	75	19, Spoon Tray	1 00
10, Electrolier	4 00	20, Ice Tea Set	3 50

Prices subject to change without notice.

...... VISITORS CORDIALLY WELCOME ......

LIBERTY CUT GLASS WORKS .·. .·. EGG HARBOR CITY, NEW JERSEY

Joe's Diner, shown in this 1924 photograph, was located at Sixth Terrace and the White Horse Pike until 1940, when it was replaced by the modern Ideal Diner. Still on its wagon wheels, the diner drew the interest of 1939 World's Fair promoters, who wanted to move it to the fairgrounds to use as a display. Owner Joseph Molasso (behind the sign) refused to move it. The Ideal Diner itself made room for the present-day Harbor Diner.

The Ideal Grill was located on the White Horse Pike between Liverpool Avenue and Fifth Terrace. Standing on the left is owner Charles Kuehnle. When he passed away a few years ago at 95 years of age, he was the area's oldest living veteran of World War I, quite a feat for one who was gassed during the war.

This building at 236 Philadelphia Avenue housed the store of J. J. Ledogar, which included an ice cream parlor and fountain service. Early in the 1900s, the double doors went to two shops, with Woerner's Tinsmith on the right. This later became the Egg Harbor Tavern (with a short-lived microbrewery), and today the building is home to the Engine 15 Tavern, featuring gourmet hamburgers, an outdoor tiki bar, and local musical talent.

Alexander's Bar and Restaurant was a popular place from the 1940s to the 1960s. It was located at the corner of Ninth Terrace and the White Horse Pike. To the left is an apartment house. Both buildings were later demolished, and the area was home to a used car lot for a time. Since around 1976, a Wawa convenience store has been located at the site.

This small shop produced a large number of the photographs contained in this book. The photography shop of Herman Kirscht was located next to his house in the 100 block of Chicago Avenue, now the site of a Wawa store. In the 1900 U.S. Census, Herman listed his occupation as a capitalist.

Just south of the Pennsylvania Railroad tracks were the livery and boarding stables of Henry W. Breder, providing carriages, horses, and ponies for rent. This photograph was taken during the city's 1905 Golden Jubilee celebration, which was the reason for the flags and bunting.

Located at Liverpool Avenue and the Reading Railroad was the firm of Winterbottom and Carter, known locally as simply the "bone mill." Samuel Winterbottom emigrated from Sheffield, England, and moved to Egg Harbor City about 1890. He started a bone knife handle business that employed 100 people. In this 1900 photograph, Winterbottom stands in front of the doorway with son Ernest to his left.

This *c.* 1930 photograph shows August Max Weiler (left) in his barbershop at 125 Philadelphia Avenue with his son Carl Albert Weiler (right). In a few years, Carl would marry Ethel Arnoldt, who lived a couple doors away. In 1940, her parents would convert the first floor into a barbershop for Carl. August's mirrors would move to the new shop where they remain today. (Roy Weiler.)

This *c.* 1895 photograph shows Laurentiam (Lorenz) Berchtold (left, beneath sign) in front of his shoe and boot store in what is part of the Kopf's Hotel building at 109 Philadelphia Avenue. Lorenz was born in the German state of Wuerttemberg and came to New Jersey in 1882. In 1888, he married Elizabeth (Lucie) Heitz of nearby Germania, believed to be the woman shown here standing to the immediate right of Lorenz.

Charles Ade's shoe repair shop adjoins Ignatz Hauser's jewelry shop at 224 and 226 Philadelphia Avenue in this *c.* 1905 photograph. The shoe shop later moved to 259 Philadelphia Avenue. The building on the right advertising a pool parlor is the Philadelphia Hotel. When the Masonic Lodge was formed, it used the hotel's second floor for its meetings and later acquired the building.

One of the larger florist operations in the area was that of Frank Obergfell, seen here in front of his store and greenhouse at 217–219 Philadelphia Avenue. This late-1920s photograph shows some of the decorative wrought iron fencing commonly found around the city until the World War II scrap drives claimed them. To the right is the house of Dr. Myrtile Frank, M.D., who became city mayor in 1929.

One of the biggest fires in Egg Harbor City's history was the Bloch Go-Cart Fire on Good Friday, 1938. It quickly raged out of control, and many fire companies were called in from as far away as Hammonton and Atlantic City to battle the several house fires caused by flying embers from the burning factory. Fire officials later determined the fire to have been ignited by the sparks from a passing train. (Thomas Hamlin.)

The boatyard of the Pacemaker Corporation (formerly C. P. Leek and Son) is seen in this *c. 1960* aerial photograph. The original building stands at the base of the bridge leading from Lower Bank. This location was used for many years to build boats of all sizes, from Charles P Leek's "sneak boxes" for hunters to large seagoing war craft such as the 72-foot English submarine chaser Q1338, built in 1944. During the Revolutionary War, John Cavileer was contracted by Gen. George Washington to build boats in what is now Egg Harbor City. Today the gravesites of John Cavileer and early settler Yoos Sooy (above the asterisk [*] near the picture's center) are maintained in front of a new sporting-boat plant that makes craft under the name of Cavileer.

In 1939, the world was on the brink of war and the United States was in need of coastal patrol boats. The 83-foot cruiser shown at right was originally built for J. Naame, but after the call was made, it was finished for the U.S. Coast Guard. The 1941 photograph below shows one of the mobile advertisements for Egg Harbor City: the 48-foot C. P. Leek and Son cruiser *Reverie II*, which used a Cummings Diesel engine and was built for F. F. Moore, president of Ryder College. Within a few months, World War II would erupt, and this placid scene off the New Jersey shore would not be repeated for four years.

This 1905 photograph of Robert Weiler's Ice Wagon shows Emil Weiler in the driver's seat and August Arnoldt Jr. on the back with a block of ice in his tongs. The location of this house has yet to be determined. This wagon is seen in several photographs of the Roundhouse Museum Collection. (Roy Weiler.)

This is the dry goods store of Max Rittenberg, located on the southeast corner of Philadelphia Avenue and the White Horse Pike. Eventually the house would be razed, and the brick building would be expanded and turned into a clothing manufacturing shop. Today the area is occupied by a gasoline station.

Three

EARLY CHURCHES

The German settlers brought religion with them, but the city was without a church during the first few years. Ulrich Günther, a Reformed Church minister, provided the spiritual needs of the residents in a nondenominational manner at Excursion Hall. The people unsuccessfully appealed to the Lutheran and the Reformed Churches to supply regular preachers. Reverend Günther suggested they send Philip M. Kleiber to the Home Mission Board of the Moravian Brethren in Bethlehem, Pennsylvania, to request a suitable clergyman. In March 1859, Rev. Christian Israel came to the city and, a year later, supervised the building of the Moravian Church and dedicated the structure on Palm Sunday 1861. Two years later, St. Nicholas German Catholic Church began construction of a church building under its first priest, Father Yunker. The Zion Lutheran Church and St. John's German Reformed Congregation began together in shared services at Excursion Hall in 1859. The Philadelphia Classis supplied Rev. J. P. Pfister for St. John's Evangelical-Reformed Church in 1862.

Other churches that followed included the First German Baptist, Emmanuel Congregational, St. Luke's AME, and Church of the Living God. Over the years, numerous other churches have appeared and then disappeared in the city; still others have been founded and successfully taken root just outside the city limits, though drawing many of their congregants from Egg Harbor City. From a single shared congregation in 1859, the area today supports a broad diversity of religious communities, reflecting the increasingly diverse population of today's Egg Harbor City. In addition to attending to the city's spiritual needs, churches have also served to bring people together with community meals, theatrical productions, sporting events, festivals, and other events. And whenever the city has needed temporary classroom space, the churches have been there to provide it.

The Moravian Church of Egg Harbor City was founded in 1859. The first services were held in Excursion Hall with Rev. Christian Israel officiating. In February 1860, it was decided to build a church, and GFTA provided five 40-by-150-foot lots on the condition that a building be completed by the end of the year. The cornerstone was laid June 27, 1860, and the dedication service was held on December 16, 1860. A two-story parsonage was built next door. A new parsonage was built in 1912, but the church remained essentially the same until 1927, when major repairs were deemed necessary. In the photograph below, the changes by Rev. Hugh Kemper are evident: stained-glass windows have been installed, stately columns added to the front, and an addition to the rear. The old parish house became a Sunday school with a large auditorium and stage on the first floor.

These two views from the early-20th century document the evolution of the Moravian church's interior. The c. 1909 photograph at right shows the high altar and central aisle of the early years, and the c. 1927 photograph below reveals radical changes in the church sanctuary: mahogany-trimmed ivory, a pipe organ, and two side aisles replacing the center aisle. Also new are the stained-glass windows, the stately columns outside, a public address system, and an expansion of the building itself, which created room for the organ.

The above 1909 image was taken from a tinted photograph looking across Philadelphia Avenue at Zion's Lutheran Church. The church stands in the center with the parsonage on the right. In later years, the church grew both out and up. The parsonage was demolished; meeting rooms and a white spire and bell tower were added. On the left in the photograph above is the church's Sunday school, which was also used by the city's Education Department. This structure was later removed, and a two-story brick apartment building erected in its place. That building today serves as home to the church's Sunday school. The 1913 photograph below shows that year's Confirmation class posed in front of the altar area. In the first row, Florence Schroeder Wiedemer stands on the far left and Julia Dey stands on the far right. The remaining confirmands are unidentified. (Author's collection / Zion's Lutheran Church.)

The above 1905 photographic postcard shows the church and parsonage of St. John's German Reformed Church in the 200 block of Washington Avenue. The church building served until the early 1930s, when a new sanctuary was constructed at London Avenue and Beethoven Street. The old building was used for basketball games (and tomfoolery by local youth) until it was demolished during World War II. The parsonage was expanded by Rev. Charles String and used until 2009, when it was sold to a church member. St. John's Consistory members were photographed on April 27, 1930, in the old sanctuary of St. John's Reformed Church on Washington Avenue. Pictured from left to right are (first row) George Friedhofer, Dr. Theodore H. Boysen, Rev. August H. Elshoff, Frederick Bange, and William Schirmer; (second row) Adolph Elmer, Joseph Heitz, Edward Meltzer, and Alex Michel. (Author's collection / St. John's UCC.)

The above photograph shows the cornerstone being set for the Sunday school part of the St. John's Evangelical and Reformed Church facing Beethoven Street on August 23, 1931, with Rev. Charles E. String officiating. From left to right, those present are Adolph Elmer, Frederick Bange, Alex Michel, Joseph Heitz, William Schirmer, two unidentified., Reverend String, Helen Boysen, unidentified., Edward Meltzer, George Friedhofer, architect Richard Shirmer, and Dr. Theodore H. Boysen, M.D. Originally the plans called for a sanctuary to be added facing London Avenue, but the Depression altered these plans. The large auditorium became a sanctuary, with folding chairs on Sunday and basketball on Monday. Finally, in the early 1950s, a permanent sanctuary was created. The interior was finished by Rudolph Rundio of St. Nicholas German Catholic Church, who reportedly needed his bishop's permission to enter the Protestant church. (St. John's UCC.)

Catholic Church and Parochial School, Egg Harbor, N. J.

The above *c.* 1905 postcard shows St. Nicholas German Catholic Church and its parochial school in the 500 block of St. Louis Avenue. At this time, the left half of the school building was the convent for parish nuns, while the priests lived in a house across the street from the church. (Notice that the church, which would burn after a 1911 lightning strike, has no lightning rods installed.) The old wooden parochial school was replaced by this modern brick building in 1928. One urban legend said that it was replaced because too many students got motion sickness during wind storms. When the church built a new rectory in 1922, the priest's house became the convent. Sadly, after more than 130 years of service, St. Nicholas Parochial School closed its doors in 2007.

This picture taken from the choir loft shows the altar in St. Nicholas German Catholic Church prior to the church's remodeling and expansion in the 1950s. During these renovations, the church railing was removed, the two statues were brought down to the expansions on their respective sides, the altar brought forward, and the walls painted in light colors.

This shows that even church buildings were subject to acts of Mother Nature. Struck by lightning in 1911, the St. Nicholas church steeple caught fire and burned with such a high heat that the bells began to melt before crashing to the floor. Insurance monies replaced the steeple; a collection replaced the bells. Some people are rumored to have taken drips from the melted bells as keepsakes. (Allen "Boo" Pergament.)

The St. Nikolaus Unterstuetzungs Verein (Benefit Association) is seen in front of the school. Standing on the left of Father Van Riehl are, from left to right, some of the early pioneers of Egg Harbor City: Andrew Dietrich, Benjamin Grawe Sr., George Sorg Sr., and Charles Kraus. Other prominent families represented here are the Butterhofs, Wennemers, Weisbeckers, Kanns, Roeschs, Berchtoldts, Engelhardts, Stadtmuellers, Gellers, and Schairers. (Ron Hesse collection.)

This c. 1915 photograph shows the new Emmanuel Congregational Church, built in 1909 at the corner of Liverpool Avenue and Agassiz Street. Notice how narrow Agassiz Street was and how both its sides were lined with trees. They were removed when the street was widened in 1921, as was the light that illuminated the intersection for safety.

The women of the St. John's Ladies Aide Society pose for this c. 1934 photograph. From left to right, they are (first row) Mathilda Flath, Frieda Englehardt, Gertrude String, Victoria Elshoff, Anna Elmer, and Marie Elmer; (second row) Laura Karrer, Katherine Michel, Daisy Kaufman, Minnie Messinger, Adele Miller, Theresa Heitz, and Sara Schirmer; (third row) Agnes Brander, Essie Karrer, Rev. Charles E. String, Mary Bauder, and Emilie Boysen. (St. John's UCC.)

The cast of one of the Moravian church's drama productions is on stage in the Moravian Hall in 1935. This produced revenue to fund the church's children's summer camps. Seen from left to right are Grace Johnson, Mina Hohneisen Pfeiffer, Irvin Weglin, Anna R Townsend, Helen Lehneis, Al Gaupp, William Pfeiffer, Eugena Johnson, Thomas Hamlin, and Mary Smith.

Four

MUSIC, SPORTS, AND ORGANIZATIONS

A favorite enjoyment of Germans and German Americans has always been music. One of Egg City Harbor's pioneers, Philip M. Wolsieffer, founded the first singing society in the United States while in Baltimore. In June 1857, even before all of the streets had been cleared in Egg Harbor City, he founded the Aurora Singing Society, an all-men's choral group that met in his house. The city enjoyed several native bands: the Egg Harbor City Band and its Junior Band, the EHC Coronet Band, the EHC Amateur Orchestra, the Turner Band, and several others. A raised bandstand was erected for the 1905 Goldenes Jubiläum in the newly dedicated Lincoln Park. Before that, small ensembles seated themselves on the tower top of Kopf's Hotel to serenade their audiences. After World War II, the all-girl St. Nick's Drum and Bugle Corps provided more homegrown musical enjoyment at parades and band competitions, and even entertained at the opening of televised professional football games.

Sports also kept Egg Harbor's citizens busy. An Egg Harbor business of even moderate size was likely to sponsor baseball, basketball, and football teams in school, church, amateur, and semiprofessional leagues. When Francis "Franny" Kern was appointed to manage the Atlantic County Detention Home facility, he used his experience as a local athlete and sports coach to form a Little League, which grew to include more than 16 grade-school-aged boys' and girls' baseball teams supported by Better-Bilt Door Company, Egg Harbor Vault Company, the Exchange Club, Sorg's Hotel, and others.

Early civic organizations in Egg Harbor included the Odd Fellows Lodge (1858) and the St. Nicholas Beneficial Society (1860). The people of Egg Harbor City also formed a Cecilia Singing Society, a Mendelsohn Club, Beethoven Society, Schiller Society, the Egg Harbor Crescendo Club, and young people's societies at nearly every church. Local residents also formed such service organizations as the Improved Order of Redmen (1902), the Daughters of Pocahontas (1903), the Pilgrim Rebekka Lodge (1899), the H. T. Dewey Lodge of the F&AM (1921), the Order of the Eastern Star, the Kiwanis Club (1922), the Grange, and the 4-H Club. Military veterans found camaraderie and support at the General Stahel Post No. 62 of the GAR, the Rudolph Elmer American Legion Post, and the Victor McAnney Post of the VFW.

In 1932, the city's Community Committee organized a 200th anniversary celebration of the birth of George Washington. Committee president William Townsend took on the role of George Washington, and U.S. postmistress Mamie Stone played Martha. This photograph was taken at the Grand Ball in Amusement Hall, located on Philadelphia Avenue. Built in 1928, Amusement Hall gradually replaced Aurora Hall as a sports center in the city. (Author's collection.)

This appears to be the Slogan Carnival Committee of 1914, shown in front of the Aurora Hotel before the parade got underway. Pictured from left to right are Aurora owner Fred Lott, Henry Cressman, two unidentified, William Schuefele, unidentified, Arthur "Snap" Mueller (with bowtie), William Brandes, unidentified, Anthony Vautrinot, William Morgenweck (with dark hat and glasses), unidentified, John Lehneis, Adolph Elmer, Christian Atz (with soft white hat), E. A. Schmidt, two unidentified, Jacob Albert, and Egg Harbor City mayor George Mueller.

Carnival Parade August 15, '14, Egg Harbor City, N. J.

These photographs continue to document the 1914 Slogan Carnival parade. Inspired by an Atlantic City event held a few weeks earlier (which produced the phrase "The World's Playground"), Egg Harbor City's 1914 Slogan Carnival resulted in the coining of the slogan, "The Ideal Spot for Your Home." While no photograph of the parade's opening section has not been found, the above photograph here shows the parade's second element: two wagons containing members of the General Stahel Post No. 62 of the GAR. Holding the flag in the first wagon is Frederick "Fritz" Boling (son of the GAR chaplain Eli Boling), who will soon find himself in the uniform of the U.S. Army on the fields of France. Riding the horse in a top hat is assistant parade marshal Jacob Albert, followed by the Cologne Coronet Band and the Lafayette Fire Department. The lower photograph shows the wagon float of the Kickapoo Tribe of the Improved Order of Redmen of Egg Harbor City, followed by members of the Patriotic Order Sons of America.

Carnival Parade August 15, '14, Egg Harbor City, N. J.

Carnival Parade August 15, '14, Egg Harbor City, N. J.

The Slogan Carnival parade continues with a decorated wagon containing members of the Cologne Grange No. 181, driven by Alex Flath. Behind this is the wagon of "The Heckers," a carriage containing the comic group know as the "Catfish Ally Band," and the Aurora Singing Society. The photograph below provides a closer view of the Aurora Singing Society float that features Rosie Mueller, daughter of Mayor George Mueller, posing as the Goddess Aurora. The trailing wagons hold the Schwaben Verein in traditional German costumes, the float of Jacob Troller featuring a giant grape juice bottle, and the Egg Harbor City Grange. (Swabia is an area of Germany in Baden-Württemberg and Bavaria that includes the Black Forest and Lake Constance, where many of the German immigrants who settled Egg Harbor City were born.)

Carnival Parade August 15, '14, Egg Harbor City, N. J.

Carnival Parade August 15, '14, Egg Harbor City, N. J.

The first wagon pictured here contains the members of the Egg Harbor City Grange, followed by a large oil tank float for the Standard Oil Company, located at Agassiz Street and Liverpool Avenue. Following this is a float for the Mueller and Mueller Coal and Lumber Company, located on Philadelphia Avenue at the railroad crossing. Behind this is the house-shaped float of house and sign painter William Spearing. Armed with the new city slogan, "The Ideal Spot for Your Home," Egg Harbor promoters proceeded to emblazon it on numerous signs and pennants, as well as the 1915 sticker below, which advertises the second annual carnival.

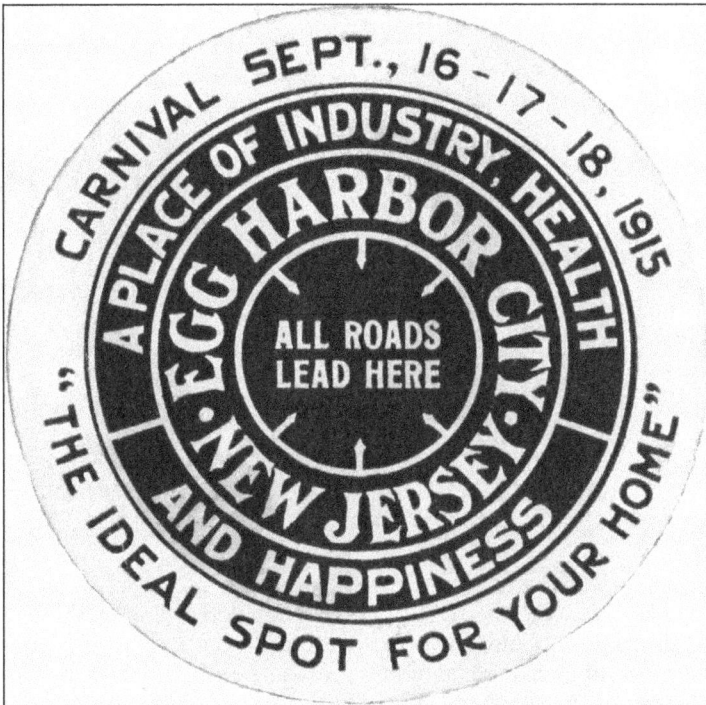

CARNIVAL SEPT., 16 - 17 - 18, 1915
A PLACE OF INDUSTRY, HEALTH AND HAPPINESS
EGG HARBOR CITY · NEW JERSEY ·
ALL ROADS LEAD HERE
"THE IDEAL SPOT FOR YOUR HOME"

This photograph from the 1915 Slogan Carnival parade at the Philadelphia Avenue and County Road (Agassiz Street) intersection looks toward the American Hotel on the left and the American Market (Acme Store) on the right. Of interest is the traffic control officer with his Stop/Go sign and the barely seen Golden Ox atop the flagpole in the center of the picture.

The women of Egg Harbor City formed a Red Cross Association during World War I that prepared bandage packets, letters from home, and other items for troops in France. Here are some of the Red Cross's members getting ready to march in a parade. Behind them is the Commercial Bank on the left and George Friz's bakery and confectionery store on the right.

The Kiwanis Club has been active in Egg Harbor City for more than 80 years. These photographs of prize-winning floats from the Armistice Day Parades of 1926 (above) and 1930 (below) show many important figures of the time. Pictured above are, from left to right (seated) former mayor Louis Garnich, William Hoffmann, Harry Rupp, unidentified, ? Karrer, Arthur Mueller, Emil Weiler, current mayor Dr. Myrtile Frank, M.D., Anthony G. Vautrinot, unidentified, William L. Karrer, unidentified, Frederick Lott, and two unidentified men; (standing) George Oberst and unidentified. The child on the float is unidentified. From left to right in the photograph below are two unidentified men, Emil Weiler, unidentified (seated in truck), ? Karrer, Al Sorg, unidentified, Dr. Myrtile Frank, Dr. Theophilus Boysen, M.D., Frederick Lott, unidentified, and William Hoffmann.

This *c*. 1912 photograph shows the Egg Harbor City Dramatic Society, one of several local theatrical groups that usually performed on the Aurora Hall stage. From left to right, the members are Elsie Neumann Frank, Edward Motz, Katherine Miller Michel, Rudolph Kroekel, Minnie Lehneis Morgenweck, Henry Gries, and Anna Lott Elmer. Katherine Miller was engaged to Edward Motz when he died in 1915 of influenza. She later married Alex Michel and was the mother of Adele Michel Baden and Ruth Ellen Michel Gronlund, who provided this photograph.

A cast photograph of the 12th-grade production *Hottentot* was taken on April 26, 1924, in Aurora Hall. From left to right are Stewart Stallnecker, Martha Morgenweck, Charles Breitzman, Daniel Michel, unidentified, Richard "Dick" Mischlich, Marie Zimmer Weiler, Albert Scheibelhut, Otto Keobler, Verna Breder, and Paul Muekser. Richard Mischlich and Marie Weiler played the leading roles, and Nellie and John Gehringer Sr. directed.

This photograph of the Egg Harbor City High School Glee Club was taken outside Public School No. 1. From left to right, they are (first row) Ralph Merkord, two unidentified, and Dorothy Todd Adshead; (second row) Dorothy Marshall Wauters, Verna Breder Warker, Henrietta Hoffman Thoms, unidentified, Martha Morgenweck Stalnecker, and Esther Todd; (third row) unidentified, Marie Zimmer Weiler, Richard Mischlich, unidentified, and Albert Scheibelhut.

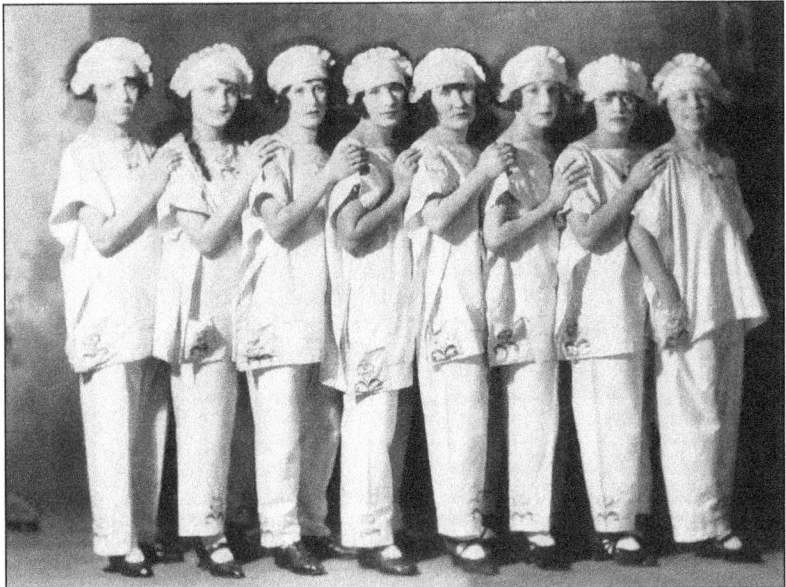

This c. 1925 photograph shows the Egg Harbor City Pajama Girls women's group dressed for the Egg Harbor City Masked Ball. From left to right, they are Flora Breder Woerner (mother of future mayor Jack Woerner), Anna Sho Haes, Sophie Haas, Magdalene Haas, Emma Soth, Irene Shouse, Lena Dampf, and Mary Rupp Gaffney.

The St. John's basketball team of 1932–1933 poses for a portrait here. From left to right are (first row) William Karrer, Clarence Schroeder, Louis Weiler, George Giesel, and Charles Breitzmann; (second row) coach John "Jack" Winterbottom, Charles Lauer, Oswald Giesel, Fred Morgenweck, and referee John V. Breitzmann Jr. In this photograph, a wire cage around the court at Amusement Hall can be seen. These cages were common to early basketball courts, which is why basketball players are even today sometimes referred to as cagers. (St. John's UCC.)

The Belmar Athletic Club was organized by coach August Keiser in 1915. Team members are, from left to right, Emeline Breder Winterbottom, Emma Kitz Wentzel, Lena Gries Jerue, Bertha Kuhnow Mueller, Helen Baum Kohnow, Rose Breder, Pauline Haas Scull, and Emma Regensburg Keiser. The club name was a brand of men's underwear manufactured by their sponsor, Baulig Underwear Company, who also made the team's navy blue uniforms and red neckerchiefs.

This photograph illustrated an *Atlantic Star Gazette* September 25, 1897, story from the 35th Annual Fair. "Among the highlights were the bicycle races. A great feature was the exhibition riding of the juveniles, Ernest Winterbottom and Henry Kuehnle Jr. These little tots made excellent time on their tandem. They have been engaged to appear at the Trenton State Fair, next week." In this photograph, Henry is on the left.

This photograph captures Jacob and Clara Dey and family members in a Durack during the 1911 Atlantic County Fair Parade in Egg Harbor City. From left to right are Catherine Van Rensallear Pfaff, Clara Dey, Tuttie Dey Frame, Jacob's mother, Jacob Dey, Paul Dey (on Jacob's lap), and William Dey. The decorated automobile—imported from France by its owner, Sen. Walter Edge—won first prize in the parade.

The Shackamaxon Council No. 51 Degree of Pocahontas, Kickapoo Tribe 237 poses for a photograph. From left to right, they are (seated) Flora Kaiser and Margaret Cope; (standing) Anna Mangold Lauer, Lena Weiss, Ruth Krable, ? Howser, Erma Walczak, Josephine Walters, Emelia Mueller, Lillian Gardner, Hettey Newman, Marguette Bader, Emolitta Sooy, Alice Henschel, Nattalie Tapken, Betty DeAngelis Sorg, Rose Breder, Rose Schlinger, Emma Winkler, Rose Henschel, Bertha Kauffman Breder Senn, Marion Michel, Mary Lehneis, Martha Tartaglione, Lillian Preidt, and Dorothy Bernhardt.

This photographic postcard shows the members of the Kickapoo Tribe 235 of the Improved Order of Redmen marching in a German Day parade in September 1906. In a note on the back to his sister-in-law, Anna Krieg, William Townsend wrote, "Probably the last German Day parade. Someone stole our beer mugs!" (Author's collection.)

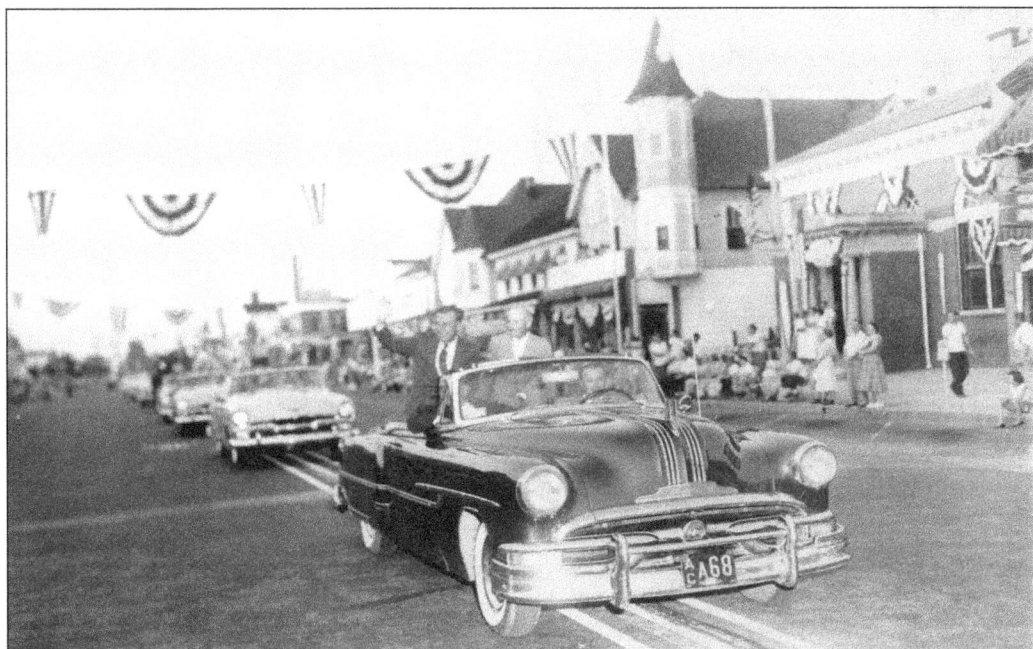

Egg Harbor City residents liked parades in 1906, and the still liked them 49 years later when the city celebrated its founding centennial in 1955. Shown above is the lead car of the parade passing city hall (the former Commercial Bank building) with New Jersey governor Richard B. Meyner on the left and Mayor W. Haines Maxwell on the right. Immediately behind are the cars of the queen (Rosemarie Pachioli) and her court.

The Germania Coronet Band formed from the Turn Gemeinde Musik Corps in 1886. Seen here, from left to right, are (first row) Louis Garnich, George Mueller Sr., Benjamin Bollman, George Karrer, George Roesch, William Haffner, and Christian Mueller; (second row) Otto Garnich, Adolph Mueller, John Fischer, Frederick Schuhardt, bandleader Jacob Oberst, unidentified, ? Keiser, Harry May, Christian Kaiser, and an unidentified man.

This photograph of the Egg Harbor City Amateur Orchestra was taken about 1900. From left to right are (seated) Ernest Shatwell, Louis Garnich, Frederick Schuhardt, Charles Cast, Herman Dietz, and George Mueller Jr; (standing) August Dey, Jacob Oberst, Harry Winterbottom, director George Mueller Sr., George Otto, and Dr. Theophillus Boysen Jr.

The Egg Harbor City Amateur Orchestra of 1905 poses for a picture. Shown from left to right are (first row, seated) William Zimmer, Jacob Oberst, George Mueller Jr. (with drum), Charles Cast, Ernest Shatwell, and Herman Dietz; (second row, standing) Hugh Meincke, William Kull, George W. Otto, Harry Winterbottom, and orchestra leader George Mueller Sr., Fred Mueller, ? Zuck, and Max Kirsch; (third row) Louis Garnich and Harry R. Rupp Sr.

One of the Egg Harbor City Band's many trips led them to the John Adams Dix GAR Post No. 135 of New York in Mount Vernon, New York. In the rear, under the bunting can be seen the members of the Egg Harbor City Band as well as the band's bass drum. General Dix was the namesake of Fort Dix, New Jersey, and father of New York governor John Alden Dix.

Among the many shows to grace the Aurora Hotel's stage was the Aurora Minstrel show on April 6, 1906. From left to right, the performers pictured are Adolph Mueller, Harry Winterbottom, Frederick Schwenger, Frederick Speyerer, two unidentified men, Harry May (white moustache), two unidentified men, director George Mueller Sr., George Mueller Jr., six unidentified men, Frank O. Breder, Fred Lott (right standing), two unidentified men, and Arthur "Snap" Mueller.

This photograph of the Egg Harbor City Coronet Band was taken for the 1905 Golden Jubilee celebration. It was taken at the Roesch's Hotel at 446–448 St. Louis Avenue. From left to right, the band members are John Roesch, George Otto, Dick Otto, Joseph Englehardt, William Friedhofer, Harry Winterbottom, August Dey, William Haffner, George Natter, August Breder, unidentified, George Sorg, Jacob Oberst, Harry Parker, Harry Rupp, Adolph Mueller, and George Roesch.

A prominent local musical group in the 1940s was Hap Brander's String Band, which toured the eastern states and Canada. From left to right are (first row) Mary Butterhof Schroer, Philip Schroer, Miriam Estalow, Charlotte Mead, Robert DeFiccio, and David Cope; (second row) Sonny Dessicino, Claire Besner, Donald Morgenweck, Marion Eivich, and Jerry Dressler; (third row) Myrtle Brander, Joan Salerno, Howard Berchtold, and "Hap" Brander; (fourth row) Raymond Mead, Charles Schlue, Carl Schneider, Clare Kurtz Schroer, and ? Herbert.

The Catfish Alley show in 1915 featured (front row, beneath stage) unidentified, Carl Weiler, Charles Schwenger, and Walter Grube; (second row) Arthur "Snap" Mueller, Adolph Mueller Sr., Joseph Braun, Harry Messinger, Fred Fraiser, unidentified, Otto Atz, Conrad Will, Herman Felter, and Charles "Coffee" Mueller; (third row) unidentified, John Felder, George Mueller, Joseph ?, Henry Kuenhle Jr., Henry Schorp, Charles Becker, Theodore Otto, and Emil Weiler.

In 1912, the city was honored by a speech stop from campaigning Theodore Roosevelt (see page 10). Twenty five years later, a king came to Egg Harbor City: John Philip Sousa, the March King. Sousa is seen here before the Lincoln Park war monuments with Egg Harbor City mayor Adolph Goller in 1927 while on his way to his annual engagement on the Steel Pier on Atlantic City's Boardwalk.

This photograph of Egg Harbor City's 1928–1929 Big Five basketball team shows, from left to right, (seated) J. Norman Kirby; (kneeling) Charles "Skin" Breitzman, Clarence "Lolly" Morgenweck, and George "Choby" Goetz; (standing) John "Stokes" Breitzman, Charles "Can" Kuehnle, Allen Bossler, Walter "Bub" Hand, Edward "Stretch" Miller, and Arthur "Snap" Mueller. After a 17-3 season, they beat a Ventnor team to win the South Jersey Championship in Aurora Hall.

This photograph of the Egg Harbor City Athletics baseball team was taken between 1902 and 1905. In the middle of the back row is pitcher Arthur "Snap" Mueller, who would shortly be off to the Single-A Eastern League. It was said that Mueller had a "snap" to his pitch, thus inspiring the nickname. He won 18 games for Toronto in the Single-A Eastern League in 1905, won 50 more over the next four years, and eventually reached AA ball in the International League in 1912, where he pitched for one year before retiring. Standing at far left is John Fisher and at far right is Harry Winterbottom.

A group of war veterans (probably American Legion members) are seen in this parade photograph from the early 1920s, possibly for Decoration Day (Memorial Day). Identified on the right end of the first row is Ernest Winterbottom. In the second row, the fifth face from the left, is Charles "Can" Kuehnle. Some of the men are armed with obsolete 40-year-old Springfield Trapdoor rifles.

The Rudolph Elmer American Legion Post 158 is seen in this 1930s photograph with a World War I cannon obtained by U.S. Rep. John Gardner. Lt. Rudolph Elmer, the youngest son of Dr. John Elmer, lost his life in the 1918 influenza epidemic while in a South Carolina training camp. Today the post building houses the Egg Harbor City Public Schools offices on Philadelphia Avenue, across from the old high school.

This 1905 photograph shows a group of boys known as the Egg Harbor City Cadets. Many of these young boys would find themselves in U.S. Army uniforms in 1917 as part of President Wilson's draft. From left to right are (first row) four unidentified boys, Charles Morgenweck, Paul von Bosse, Charles Kuehnle, unidentified, Frederick Winterbottom, and Gustave Riedel; (second row) Theodore Messinger, Rudolph Elmer, Louis Kuehnle, ? Kitz, William Vogel, and three unidentified boys; (third row) four unidentified boys, George Christ, and unidentified.

The Egg Harbor City Vikings were the Atlantic County Champions in 1935. Shown from left to right in this picture taken at the Egg Harbor City Fairgrounds are (first row) Elmer Kienzle, Matthew Cairone, George Sciore, Lawrence Lauer, Leonard Stump, Anthony Sciore, and William Berggoetz; (second row) Moe Nehr, George Breder, Peter Cairone, August Dey, John Ade, unidentified, Charles Werner, Clarence "Lolly" Morgenweck, and George Ade.

This 1887 photograph is identified as the Turner Coronet Band, Egg Harbor City. Probably the oldest musical organization in the state, the band was founded in 1860. Of interest are the large horns called "back-horns" because the horn's bell faced the rear when played. The band eventually was renamed the Germania Coronet Band and then Egg Harbor City Band. The c. 1890 photograph below shows, from left to right, orchestra members (front row) Joseph Englehardt, Joseph Englehardt Jr., Harry Berchtold, William Berchtold, Christian Atz, and Jacob Dey; (second row) George Natter, Louise Atz Hemphill, Marie Elmer, Mr. Hemphill, Sophie Sauer, Rose Sharp, and Carl Heniss; (third row) Emil Morgenweck, William Sykes, Frank Frazer, Fred Morgenweck, John Ade, George Soth, John Loedegar, and Charles Dihlmann; (fourth row) Henry Wimberg, William Sauer, Charles Englehardt, Frederick Schuhardt, and Lorenz Berchtold.

Many bands had their beginning in the school, like the Egg Harbor City High School Dance Band of 1955. Shown here from left to right are (first row) Ralph Debauch, Joseph Heitz, Edwards Haas, Frederick Son, William Reiter, William Bange, and William Walters; (second row) instructor Harling Darling and pianist Hazel Browne. Below is the 1955 EHC High School Band. From left to right, they are (first row) Velda Patton, Julia Priest, Frances Barrett, Mary Knisell, and Dorothy Priest; (second row) William Swanfield, Andrew James, Leo Reynolds, Wheatley Wall, Ralph Edelbach, Walter Jennigan, Anthony Ruberton, and Fanny Sampayo; (third row) Ned Jacob, William Walters, Stanley Eklar, Frances Previte, William Pfeiffer, William Hamilton, Edwin Spragg, and Claude Comforti; (fourth row) Robert Luke, Daniel Berkowitz, James Ryan, Hazel Brown, Fred Sohn, and Ed Haas; (fifth row) Joseph Heitz, Harling Darling, and John Vetter.

The Veterans of Foreign Wars was organized as the Victor McAnney Post No. 5341 and bought the old Commercial Bank Building to convert it into the home post. This photograph was taken at the dedication in 1952 and shows the members of the St. Nicholas Girls Drum and Bugle Corps and color guard.

On the right is Capt. Charles Saalman amongst his grapes at the Black Rose Vineyard. Captain Saalman returned from the Civil War partially disabled with a severe left arm wound suffered in battle at Gettysburg while serving with the 75th Pennsylvania Infantry. On his left is fellow veteran Wilhelm Krieg who was also wounded at Gettysburg while in the 27th Pennsylvania Volunteers. (Author's collection.)

This is the farm of Capt. Charles Saalman, the home of the Black Rose Vineyard. Located outside the city limits on Darmstadt Avenue, this was one of the larger, well-respected vineyards in the area. Saalman bought the property after the Civil War, and it still remains in the family. Captain Saalman's son William became a lawyer and also sang. Numerous radio stations, including WFPG in Atlantic City, featured his baritone voice in the early 1930s.

This is the Egg Harbor City Fife and Drum Corps, c. 1895, under the direction of Hugh Meincke. Shown from left to right are (first row) August Lesemann, John Woerner, and Frederick Christ; (second row) William Davis, ? Gries, unidentified, Harry Winterbottom, Louis Woerner, and Hugh Meincke.

The 1957 St. Nicholas All-Girls Drum and Bugle Corps prepares for the year ahead. Each year a photograph was taken for use on their event programs. A well-known unit, they played in President Eisenhower's 1956 Inaugural Parade and at the 1960 Democratic Convention, opened a National League football game, and had an audience with Francis Cardinal Spellman following a New York City St. Patrick's Day parade. The corps also hosted an annual competition held in the Atlantic City convention hall that attracted corps from the entire mid-Atlantic region. The members' uniforms in this picture were bright gold and dark green with the drum majorettes in white. At left is manager Michael Jiampetti with drum majorette Maddy Champion behind him. At right is Father Stoerlein with drum majorette Kathy Mattle behind him. Also identified in the picture are Diane DeLuca (above left of Father Stoerlein), Betty Toma Kobelo (second row between first two drummers), Florence Toma (left behind Maddy Champion), and Barbara Dampf (first row, fourth drummer). Their summertime evening practice in the school yard brought out many onlookers and rounds of applause.

Many football teams were formed at the end of the 19th century, such as this group of players seen near the train station at Philadelphia Avenue and Atlantic Street. Shown here from left to right are (first row) Harry Kumpf, Henry "Pop" Kuehnle, Edward Motz, William "Standpipe Bill" Sauer, James Cavaluccia, John Henry Yanko, and Al "Morge" Morgenweck; (second row) John Winterbottom, George Wolsieffer, Ernest Winterbottom (crouching down), and unidentified.

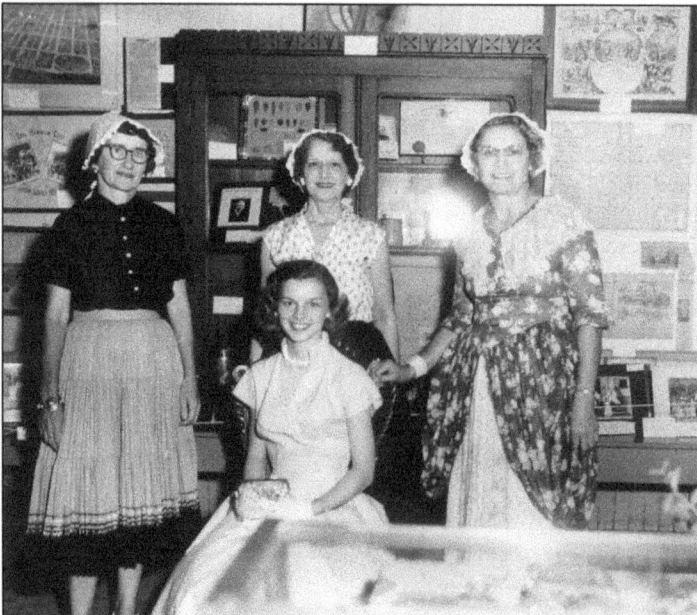

During Egg Harbor City's 1955 centennial, the celebration committee oversaw the creation of a one year historical exhibit at the city library in the Lafayette Fire House. In 1990, resurgent interest in local history led to the creation of the Roundhouse Museum, and many items seen in this 1955 photograph now share a single home once again. From left to right are (seated) Centennial Queen Rosemarie Pachioli; (standing) Anna R. Townsend, Myrtle Kears, and Esther Elmer.

Five

PUBLIC SERVICES

Egg City Harbor's German immigrant founders were strong proponents of public education. To this end, they erected the multipurpose Excursion Hall, which, in addition to serving as a meeting place for rail excursions and religious worship, provided a place to hold school classes. Public School No. 1 was built in 1876 for $6,586.80; at the time, it was the largest and most modern school in Atlantic County. It expanded in 1895 and again in 1917. In 1923, the Egg Harbor City High School was built, and in 1928, St. Nicholas German Catholic Church replaced its wooden school with a large brick building. After World War II, classroom space was limited; Buffalo Avenue School was built in 1955 to serve kindergarten through third grade while the Pike School took the remaining grades. In 1960, Oakcrest Regional High School was constructed, and the old EHCHS building became the Philadelphia Avenue School when the Pike School was demolished. At publication, a new middle school is being built, and high school students who had moved to Absegami will soon attend the new Cedar Creek High School.

Not only were Egg Harbor City's fathers concerned about education, but they were also concerned about safety. Accordingly, the Egg Harbor City council allocated $500 for a fire department in 1858, though Lafayette Hose Fire Company No. 1 did not appear until November 1880. The city's first firefighting apparatus—beyond the faithful bucket—was a hand-drawn "pitcher pump." In 1887, the city obtained its first firefighting vehicle, a used hand-drawn ladder truck. Since "Good Will Hook and Ladder Company" was already stenciled in gold on the truck, Egg Harbor City firefighters adopted the name. In 1913, Chemical Engine Company No. 1 was added. Fire Chief Henry W. Breder suggested a merger into a single fire department, and a new fire station was built for this consolidated department in 1918.

Crime was not a major concern in the earliest days of the city, when city marshal George Senft policed the city on his bicycle. By 1930, however, the city had a police chief with three officers. The county took over the former dormitory of Dr. Smith's spa for a juvenile detention center, and later created the Harborfields Detention Center. The police also manned the volunteer ambulance service that started up after World War II. Prior to the purchase of the city's first designated ambulance, one of the Wimberg funeral hearses doubled for one.

The Egg Harbor City Health Department was created early in the city's history and worked with the Board of Education to create the first schools in Atlantic County with a permanent school nurse and regular medical and dental visits.

This is the earliest known photograph of Public School No. 1. Note the absence of the ventilators seen in later photographs. When it was constructed in 1876, this was the largest school building in Atlantic County, and school administrators from around the state visited to observe its many innovative features. It featured central heating and contained six classrooms, including one that had a folding wall to divide it into two smaller rooms.

This photograph was taken from Buffalo Avenue and Steuben Place behind the Good Will firehouse in 1905. The 1896 addition to Public School No. 1 contained three classrooms and restroom facilities, helping to divide classes into single-grade rooms, but there was still a classroom shortage. Ventilators can now been seen on the roof of the 1876 building section.

This photograph shows the final form of Public School No. 1. It was expanded about 1917 with the addition that mirrored the front of the building and was known as "the colored school," later designated School No. 3. Four rooms were added for the segregated grade-school classes, which continued until the early 1950s. While the lowered grades were segregated, the three high school classes were integrated.

Anna Townsend's first-grade class of 1953 is seen outside the "Little Yellow Schoolhouse" (School No. 4). Located on the west side of the 500 block of Philadelphia Avenue, the building had three rooms, each with a coal stove, and two bathrooms, entered by exterior doors. Other classes at this time were Miss Barnes's second grade and Miss Devine's kindergarten. (Author's collection.)

Egg Harbor City Souvenir

CITY HALL—During Golden Jubilee

annie we cannot come up saturday
will write later Louisa 11-20-1905

The Lafayette Fire House (pictured here in 1905), like its successor, served double duty as city hall on the second floor. Located at Cincinnati Avenue and Buerger Street, the structure was recently refurbished with a historical building grant and continues to serve the public as a senior citizens center. It has also been a school classroom, a library, and a museum for the city's 1955 centennial celebration. (Author's collection.)

Here is an early fire company dressed for a parade. These are the two earliest hand pumps owned by the companies. The 1860 pitcher pump on the right had a 1.25-inch hose fed by the pump from the water reservoir filled by a bucket brigade. The pump on the left was purchased a few years later. Originally a hand-drawn pump, the horse was added later.

The seat of city government moved several times from Excursion Hall to the present building on London Avenue. The next to the last stop was the former Commercial Bank building on Philadelphia Avenue. During this time, the building suffered its only robbery when thieves broke in at night to rob the vault. The vault firmly resisted for hours, and they finally settled for the City Lake Park receipts box.

This is the Egg Harbor City Police Department of the 1920s. Chief Philip J. Reinhard stands beside the police car in front of the firehouse on Philadelphia Avenue that housed the courtroom/Common Council meeting room on the second floor. At the front of the car is officer George Roesch, and at the rear of the car is officer Edward Camillo.

One of several buildings that served as the post office in Egg Harbor City was this one located on the southeast side at 118 Philadelphia Avenue. It was located here until about 1922 when it moved across the street to the north side of the new Broadway Building where it shared the first floor with the A&P store.

The back portion of this building is the original water department structure erected in 1897. Together with a network of service mains and the "reservoir" at Philadelphia Avenue and Buerger Street, the city had an effective water distribution system for use by the people and the fire department. The front section was added in the early 1950s to provide space for larger pumps.

The Egg Harbor City Fire Department rolled out its equipment for this photograph used in the 1930 Diamond Jubilee booklet. They are identified from left to right with their trucks. Pictured with the Hahn Ladder truck are Martin Stutzbach, George Heniss (driver), George Blase, Charles Christ, George Soth, Bill Roesch, Fred Meinecke, Joseph Berninger, George Zimmer, and Ernest Gaupp; with the small Ford hose-pumper truck are August Bader, Emil Weiler, Fred Michel (driver), George Schieder (next to driver), Joseph Williman (left rear), and Richard Lobherr (right rear); with the small Ford hose-pumper truck are Adolph Mueller, Fire Chief Henry Breder, Hugh Meincke, William Keiser (driver), Fredrick Ade (left of driver), August Breder (left rear), and Otto Weiler (right rear); and with the Ford utility truck are Charles "Snap" Mueller, Harry Breder (driver), Louis Garnich (next to driver), John Breder, Jacob Albert, William Ruch, August Keiser (left rear), Louis Bauer (right rear), and William Kaiser. The firehouse and A&P would remain at these locations until the late 1960s, The American Store at the left edge of the photograph would move in 1934, and Otto's Stationery shop would continue for a few more years after that.

The Egg Harbor City Fire Department posed for this picture at Lafayette Fire House about 1900. From left to right are (first row) unidentified, Otto Weiler, unidentified, fire marshal Henry Wimberg, George Roesch, Frederick Berchtold, George Blasé, and unidentified; (second row) two unidentified, August Breder, unidentified, Henry Wehming, John Fisher, Jacob Dey, and unidentified; (third row) Emil Heniss, Adolph Goller, Henry Wimberg, and Frederick Schwenger. In the c. 1913 photograph below is the Egg Harbor City Chemical Engine No. 1. It used the reaction of baking soda with acid to create gas under pressure to force water through the hose. Identified on the right are August Dey, Capt. George Zimmer, and Chief Henry Breder.

Chemical Engine Co. No. 1, Egg Harbor City, N. J.

This c. 1910 photographic postcard shows the Good Will Hook and Ladder Company firehouse that faced Agassiz Street and was located across Buffalo Avenue from Lincoln Park. In the distance behind the firehouse is the back end on the Liberty Cut Glass factory.

The members of the Egg Harbor City Fire Department are shown here participating in the bicentennial celebration of the Relief Fire Company of Mount Holly, New Jersey, on July 12, 1952. The picture shows their Mack pumper truck, and nestled above the helmets and boots can be seen the 1860 pitcher pump.

The first new school construction since the high school was built in 1923 was the Buffalo Avenue School in 1955, for kindergarten through fourth grades. Recently expanded and upgraded, the total cost of the original nine-classroom school was $155,009.85. The multimillion-dollar facility of today includes special education, a library, and a multipurpose hall.

This photograph of the fire department's ladder truck was taken prior to a formal department photograph (seen on page 95) for use in the 1930 book of the Diamond Jubilee celebration of the city's founding. This truck was finally retired in the 1950s when it was replaced with another ladder truck with large water tanks.

Six

SITES AND LANDMARKS

Each city or town has its landmarks, and Egg Harbor City is not wanting. Though some landmarks have been lost to fire or obsolescence—the Welcome Arch over County Road, the Renault Bottling Plant, Public School No. 1, and the many clothing factories that made the city grow still exist today. Most notable is the giant champagne bottle at the edge of town on US-30, advertising the L. N. Renault Winery. The winery once had multiple bottles in New Jersey, New York, and California, but of these, only four bottles remain—and only two of these serve their original purpose. Dr. Smith's Neutral Water Health Resort Sanitarium, well-known from Baltimore to New York City, used the "cedar water" of a local stream; the spa's former site is now home to Peace Pilgrim Park, the Municipal Building, and the Roundhouse Museum. The Egg Harbor City Lake Park, built and once owned by Dr. Smith, continues to provide a refreshing break from the summer heat. The one-time Excursion Park, renamed in honor of President Lincoln, is one of two sites for honoring Egg Harbor City's military veterans. It also hosts the annual "Cruisin' to the Beach" antique auto show, the Hometown celebration, Oktoberfest, and Christmas celebration. Throughout Egg Harbor City, many 1800s buildings and homes remain, including an early GFTA brick house at Havana Avenue and Diesterweg Street. The Commercial Bank building and Dr. Smith's Vapor House have taken on new uses as, respectively, the Egg Harbor City branch of the county library and the Roundhouse Museum. Both of these buildings are official New Jersey State Historic Sites. Soon to join them is the Lafayette Fire House/city hall building. The town is also fortunate to have a fleet of mobile landmarks in the form of many surviving boats built by Egg Harbor Boat, C. P. Leek and Son, Ocean Yacht, and Pacemaker Corporation. Some of Egg Harbor City's landmarks, both present and past, are pictured on the following pages.

Gedenkblatt der Gründung von
EGG HARBOR CITY

This is the earliest known image of Egg Harbor City, a lithograph made from an ambrotype taken by A. Morhart in April 1858 and prepared by F. Wogram, 54 Chatham Street, New York City. The central focus of the image is the Camden and Atlantic Railroad and Atlantic Street between Washington and Buffalo Avenues. On the left is the GFTA Egg Harbor City Hotel built over Third Terrace between Washington and London Avenues. Its location is the reason the city water pipes stopped before reaching the end of the terrace. Next is Louis Kuehnle's original New York Hotel at Liverpool Avenue across the tracks from the C&A Railroad "station." Across the street is Ertell's Hotel that later became Aurora Hotel. The building on the east side of Philadelphia Avenue is the Neuhaus property, to the right, and beneath a pennant is Excursion Hall in Excursion Park.

1921

This aerial photograph from early 1921 shows much of the "downtown" area of Egg Harbor City. In the lower half is the fairgrounds, the Liberty Cut Glass and Baulig Underwear factories, and Public School No. 1. The Good Will firehouse had been removed, but the school yard fence was not yet extended to Buffalo Avenue. The large house across the Pike belonged to Theodore Baulig. In the center are Lincoln Park and the Atlantic City Gas Plant. Along Philadelphia Avenue near the tracks is the white Shindel, Stern Clothing factory, across Sixth Terrace from Mueller's Lumber and Coal Yard. The new Broadway Building is seen north of the White Horse Pike. Also visible are the major transportation arteries: the White Horse Pike on the right, Philadelphia Avenue/Mays Landing Road in the middle, the Pennsylvania-Seashore Line on the left, and the Reading Railroad in the upper left corner, running past the Samuel Winterbottom's "bone mill." Note that the Welcome Arch has yet to be built across the Pike at Lincoln Park. At top center is the smokestack of the Atlantic County Electric Company.

This ink and water color rendition of Excursion Hall shows the building as it was remembered by local artist George W. Otto in the 1950s. No known photograph remains of Excursion Hall, the multipurpose building used as a meeting house for government and church services as well as a school. It was demolished after 1876 when Public School No. 1 was opened. (Author's collection.)

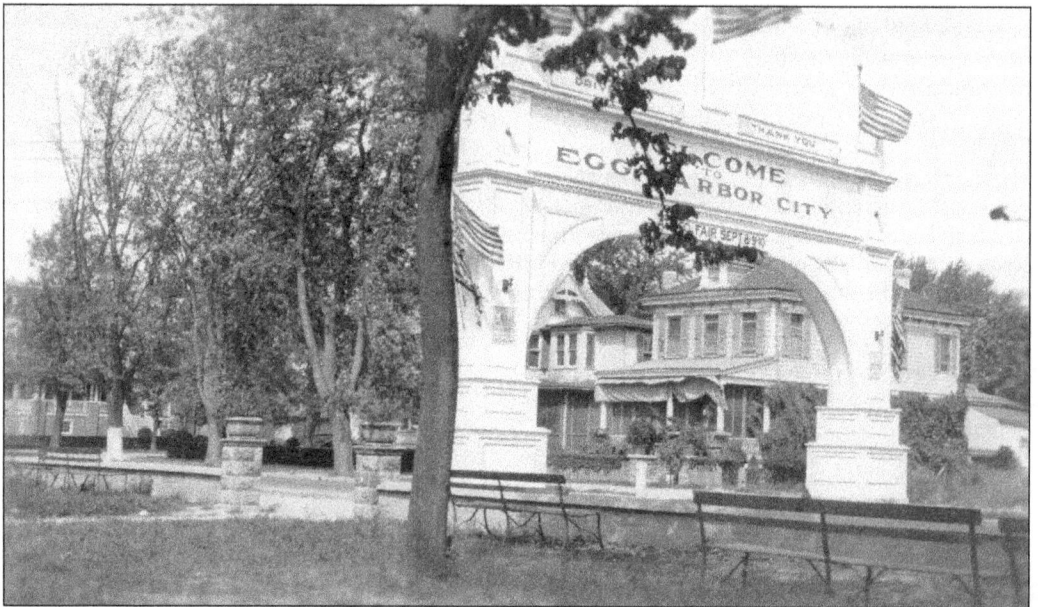

The Welcome Arch was built in the spring of 1921 at the center entrance to Lincoln Park during the widening of Agassiz Street. Then known as County Road, in 1928 the street was turned over to the state and became the White Horse Pike and US-30. A further widening of the road led to the loss of the Welcome Arch and several feet on either side of the roadway.

Shown here are the two sites of the city's annual Memorial Day services. Above is the Civil War monument in the Egg Harbor City cemetery, seen in this *c.* 1898 photograph with members of the General Stahel Post No. 62 of the GAR. From left to right are ? Guthlein, William Hohneisen, Joseph Schwiekerath, F. Waschow, unidentified, Henry Voss, unidentified, William Mischlich, Louis Ertell, Gustave Guenther, John Prasch, Jacob Natter, William Morgenweck, Joseph Englehardt (son of Charles Engelhardt), and Eli Bolling. Below is a view of the Egg Harbor City soldiers' memorial in Lincoln Park, honoring local residents who served during one or both of the world wars. The World War I obelisk was dedicated April 3, 1920, and the World War II flanking memorials were erected in 1946. Memorials for Korea and Vietnam have since been added.

Artist Theodore H. Gloeckner's *Sketches in Egg Harbor, N. J.* shows some of the scenes about town in 1888. Included are two churches, the fairgrounds between Chicago and St. Louis Avenues on Agassiz Street, Kuehnle's New York Hotel on Philadelphia Avenue, the city hall/Lafayette Fire House, Good Will firehouse, and the schoolhouse. Confirming the date is the Goebels Block building with the Commercial Bank sign on it. (Ruth Ellen Gronlund.)

In 1905, the 50th anniversary of the founding of Egg Harbor City, Excursion Park was renamed Lincoln Park in honor of the great president. A fountain in a large basin was presented to the city by George Gerlach, and a bandstand was constructed on the site of Excursion Hall. Today the fountain can be seen at the Roundhouse Museum (see page 127).

This early 1900s view of Philadelphia Avenue toward Agassiz Street shows Kopf's Hotel building and Lorenz Berchtold's shoe store. The flagpole in the center of the block is at the post office, and the third flagpole is at the GAR Post No. 68. On the back of the card, someone has written: "Peter Michel turning into Philadelphia Avenue with flat bed wagon." Marshall George Senft, in uniform, is on the left. (Ruth Ellen Gronlund.)

This is another early 1900s view of the 100 block of Philadelphia Avenue from the opposite direction. From left to right are Kopf's Hotel building with Berchtold's shoe store at the far end, the Arnoldt family house, the Reichenbach house, and the Cigar Shop. The space between Kopf's and Arnoldt's later became Arnoldt's Butcher Shop. (Ruth Ellen Gronlund.)

This photograph was taken during the 1917 Annual Gymnastics Day exercises held on the grounds of Public School No. 1. Children from first grade through high school took part in this annual activity until it was discontinued during World War II. Beyond the children is the Good Will firehouse and Lincoln Park.

This is a northerly view of the Butterhof farmhouse and Chestnut Grove Vineyard, taken from the south entrance road near Agassiz Street. Founded in 1854, the vineyard is not within the Egg Harbor City limits but was part of the original GFTA tract. It is still operated by the Butterhof family today, producing flowers, fruits, and vegetables that are sold from a roadside stand. The house can easily be seen from US-30.

This is a winter view of Dr. Smith's Neutral Water Health Resort Sanitarium on London Avenue seen from the observation tower. In the center is the main hotel with a pump house/mill to the left across the serpentine creek. The building above the bridge at the far left is the Egg Harbor City Water Company. The 16-sided building is now the Roundhouse Museum. Many of the houses in the background still exist today.

Here is a group of people at Dr. Smith's doing what they were supposed to do here. Dr. Smith reasoned that the cedar waters of this creek revitalized the body and cured its ills, so what better way was there to get exercise than by walking against the current, no matter what time of year? (Yes, that is snow on the ground and in the water.)

The Bungalow Hotel was built by Dr. Smith on the north side of the Egg Harbor City Lake to serve lake visitors. Throughout the years it has had several owners and catered to many different groups. It was known to have the best venison burgers in town during the Depression years. It has recently been renovated by the owner of Renault Winery for use by his important guests.

Halfway between the Bungalow Hotel and the Shaler gravesite on the northeast side of the city lake was the roundhouse pavilion. A favorite place for summertime parties, dances, concerts, clambakes, and outdoor church services, this cedar-shake building was lost to vandals in the 1960s and replaced by a low-walled, open-air concrete block pavilion.

The city's greatest urban legend revolves around this secluded gravesite. Sibbel Shaler, the wife of Revolutionary War privateer Timothy Shaler, died April 2, 1785, aged 34 years, and was buried here with her three "infant children." There is no clear evidence of the cause of death, but the unfounded legend is that they were massacred by Native Americans. Unfortunately (for the story), the state has no record of Native American troubles . . . ever.

This is a view of the northeast end of the Egg Harbor City Lake. Seen here is the concrete bulkhead and dam built by Dr. Smith after vandals destroyed the original wooden dam. Beyond the dam is a sawmill that was a popular place for outings and several period photographs. Farther downstream, the water entered Gloucester Lake then flowed on to the Mullica River.

A group of children are seen in front of one of the changing buildings, enjoying the cool refreshing cedar water at the Egg Harbor City Public Bath while a few adults look on. This was a concrete-lined pool with free-flowing water from one of the several creeks in the city, located at Buerger Street and New Orleans Avenue.

The old city jail has seen better days, even as it sports a new roof. Long ago relegated to being a storage building, it has had its moments. In 1918, a large group of rowdy army boys from the ammunition plant at Amatol found themselves in this lockup. It is said that once they calmed down, they literally raised the roof so they could get back for roll call.

This *c.* April 1927 photograph was taken at 456–458 Philadelphia Avenue in front of the Will's Bavarian Hotel. The subject of the photograph is Walter Yeager, who had a print shop in the 100 block of Chicago Avenue. The man on the porch is Robert Will. The building looks much the same today, but is now a two-family house.

Originally constructed as the office for the Bullinger Agency, the realtors that handled the sale of city properties, this is one of the oldest surviving buildings in the city. Following the Civil War, it served for a while as an orphanage for war veterans' children before becoming a family residence. Barely seen on the far left is the kiln building of the porcelain works on London Avenue.

Erected in 1859, this building was known as the piano factory. Though built to entice the Schumacher Piano Factory into moving here from Philadelphia, for years, the only thing manufactured here was shoes. The building later served as an agricultural school. It was derelict for years and demolished in 1895. An electric light generating plant was built on its foundation. Today the site is home to a transformer substation.

Phila. Ave Looking North, Egg Harbor, N. J.

This mid-1920s postcard shows two new buildings on Philadelphia Avenue just north of Agassiz Street. Left of center is the firehouse/city hall building. The former Kopf's Egg Harbor Hotel building to the right has been torn down, and Howard H. Bozarth has built the Broadway Building in its place, with the A&P on the left and post office on the right. The second floor contained three apartments, and the third floor was used by the Masonic Order.

The Hotel Atlantic stood at the north corner of Philadelphia Avenue and Beethoven Street until the late 1950s. It was one of the last hotels in the city to be razed for new construction. Shortly afterward, people began saving the old buildings to become restaurants, taverns, or apartments. Today the local telephone exchange occupies this spot.

HOTEL ATLANTIC
WM. SUYKERS, Prop.
Cor. Beethoven and Philadelphia Avenues   EGG HARBOR CITY, N. J.

Katherine Kumpf's New York Hotel was located on the corner of Philadelphia Avenue and Atlantic Street, across from the Pennsylvania Railroad station. Originally built by Charles Kumpf on land formerly owned by Louis Kuehnle, it is not to be confused with Kuehnle's New York Hotel (see page 100). Note the Christian Atz Lager Beer sign on the right.

This 1950s photograph shows Joe's Diner, a house, and a gas station where the Egg Harbor Diner is today. The garage at the bottom right and Dr. Boysen's drugstore were removed to build an Eckerd Drug store. The auto repair garage above it became an Exxon station. Egg Harbor Lumber closed a few years later, and a half-covered railroad siding remains, as does the center group of buildings.

In the late 1950s, Egg Harbor City planners decided to replace the old black "water reservoir" at the corner of Buerger Street and Philadelphia Avenue with a higher, modern steel ball-type tank on pedestal legs—seen here in May 1962. Work on the new tank began by driving steel beams to create the leg bases behind the Lafayette Fire House. Also seen is one of the fire sirens used to call the city's volunteer firemen.

Seven

THE PEOPLE

The inhabitants of Egg Harbor City came from far and wide. A review of the old tax and census records show that they came from America's large cities; its small towns; the German-speaking states of Württemberg, Hesse, Prussia, and Alsace-Lorraine; France; and Switzerland. Many were dedicated to the concept put forward by the GFTA, and several proved their faithfulness by continuing to pay their taxes to the GFTA during the Civil War while they fought in Georgia, Virginia, and the Carolinas. The 1900 U.S. Census recorded that more than 50 percent of Egg Harbor City's inhabitants listed their birthplace in German-speaking European countries.

Other ethnic groups followed, hearing of the haven in the pines of New Jersey. English mill workers, former slaves, and the children of slaves, Italian rail workers, eastern Europeans, Hispanics, and Asians made their way to Egg Harbor City to build new lives. A few became known well beyond the city's borders through their abilities in sports, show business, or politics. And for every one Egg Harbor City resident who became known to the world, there were many, many neighbors who had helped them to reach the heights they reached: coaches, teachers, family members, and friends. Egg Harbor City has always attracted and produced good people. The following photographs represent but a fraction of them.

P. M. Wolsieffer
FIRST MAYOR

Francis Bierwirth
FIRST ELECTED MAYOR

Philip Mathias Wolsieffer was appointed the first mayor of Egg Harbor City by the directors of the GFTA. Coming to Egg Harbor City at the beginning, Wolsieffer was instrumental in creating the city's musical organizations. He had founded the first singing society in the United States while in Baltimore and started the second one (Aurora) in Egg Harbor City. Recently discovered carbon copies of his record books show that he was also a business manager with strong perseverance. His descendants inherited this trait and his love for music. His son wrote a funeral march used for Lincoln's funeral, and a great-granddaughter became world-known as "Peace Pilgrim." In 1861, Francis Bierwirth was the first mayor elected by popular vote, serving but a short time before enlisting in the 27th Pennsylvania Volunteer Infantry. He was later transferred and became a captain in the 69th Pennsylvania Volunteer Infantry. He was killed and buried at Antietam.

August Stephany was a driving force in the commercial well being of the Egg Harbor City area. He founded the Stephany Insurance Agency in Egg Harbor City and later in Atlantic City. He was a founder of the Commercial Bank of Egg Harbor City, organized the Egg Harbor City Kiwanis Club in 1922, and was a member of the Aurora Singing Society.

Christian Atz was the founder of the largest brewery in Egg Harbor City. He owned several lots in the 400 block of Philadelphia Avenue, where he built his house and the Atz Brewery. With brewmaster Conrad Will, Atz developed a popular cedar water beer. The brewery's name was later changed to Egg Harbor Brewery, and the house and brewery buildings remain today.

This card asked everyone to come help sing "The Schnitzel Bank" at "Coffee" Mueller's Rathskeller, located at 521 Liverpool Avenue. At the piano is Don Ireland, with Mueller pointing to the board. On the back of the card is an invitation to "Bub's Birthday Party" on Saturday May 26, 1930, with a chicken salad lunch. In this picture, Charles "Bub" Mueller is playing the guitar.

David Franklin Cavileer, seen in his U.S. Army uniform, liked to tell the story of a run-in he had with Gen. George Patton. As an MP, he stopped Patton's car for an oncoming Red Ball Express. Afterwards, when the car slowly passed Cavileer, Patton told the driver, "Remember him, and next time you see him, run over the SOB." David's favorite duty, for over 50 years, was playing Santa Claus for many friends' children—and their children.

One of the city's more prominent African American families is represented here by Larkey Mays III, Larkey Mays Jr., and Larkey Mays Sr. The senior Larkey was one of the founders of the local Church of the Living God. His son worked at Nurre Mirror and was an accomplished welder. Larkey Mays III completed his degree at University of Massachusetts in three years and worked for many years at Rohm and Haas in Philadelphia. (Connie Bennett Mays.)

Willie Earl Phillips is pictured here in his Second Cavalry uniform as he served his country during World War II. His son William received a bachelor of arts degree and retired as a school social worker; Lenora received a bachelor of arts and masters of social work degree, and also retired as a school social worker. She married Jesse Edmonds, the city's first black Board of Education president. Willie's second daughter Marsha holds bachelor of science and master of science degrees and is teaching nutrition at area colleges. (Lenora Edmonds.)

A smiling John Gilly, superintendent of Public Schools, stands before the picture of predecessor Charles L. Spragg at the ribbon-cutting ceremony for the expansion of the Spragg School in August 2009. Spragg came here in 1949 from Tuckerton after the resignation of William Miller. He retired in 1977, and in 1994, the Buffalo Avenue School was renamed in his honor.

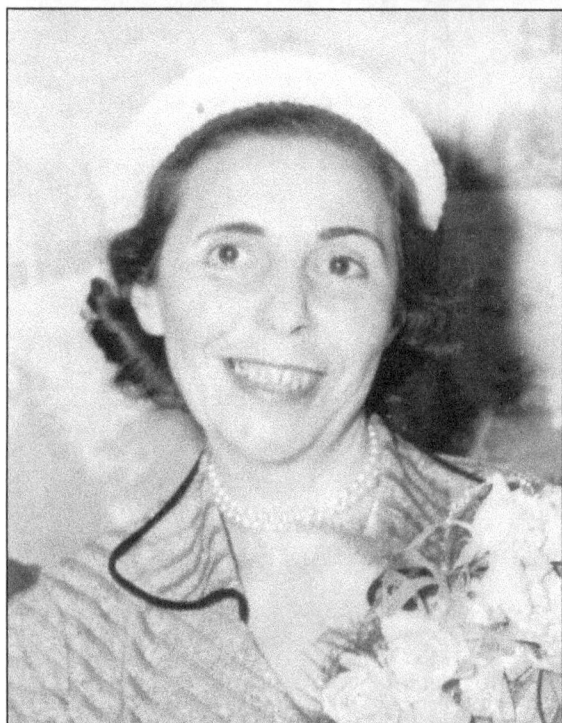

Fanny D. Rittenberg was a longtime teacher and a supervising principal of Egg Harbor City High School. Whether it was drilling the Gettysburg Address into her students' memories or encouraging the talents of world-recognized artist Ned Jacob, she was always there for her students. After retirement, the Philadelphia Avenue School (formerly Egg Harbor City High School) was renamed in her honor.

Antoinette Doell was born in 1876, the year Public School No. 1 was built. She was a student, teacher, and principal in the Egg Harbor City schools. In 1954, she began a series of historical columns for *The News* in preparation for the city's centennial, reproduced in the 1955 celebration booklet. She was also named Egg Harbor City's 1955 Citizen of the Year.

This 1895 photograph shows Harry May (1855–1946) in his Egg Harbor Knights of the Golden Eagle Band uniform. May had a dry goods store and did canning (see page 39), and one of his recipes was sold and later became the recipe used for Campbell's Pork and Beans. (Harry Jensen family collection.)

The family of "Commodore" Louis Kuehnle was well respected in the county. He owned the New York Hotel on Liverpool Avenue and more properties both here and in Atlantic City. His son Henry turned the hotel into his home, as seen in the background. Grandsons Louis and Charles Kuehnle are in the front and Fredrick Winterbottom in the rear of the pony cart, preparing to join the Golden Jubilee parade in 1905.

The Egg Harbor High School class of 1909 consisted of Clarence Nice, Christian Mueller, Hanson Hamilton, Florence Roesch, Lena Zimmer, Emily Koch, Laura Emmer, Carrie Ledogar, Frieda Thoms, Ellie Miller, and Viola Boysen. The bespectacled Viola was the daughter of Dr. Theo Boysen.

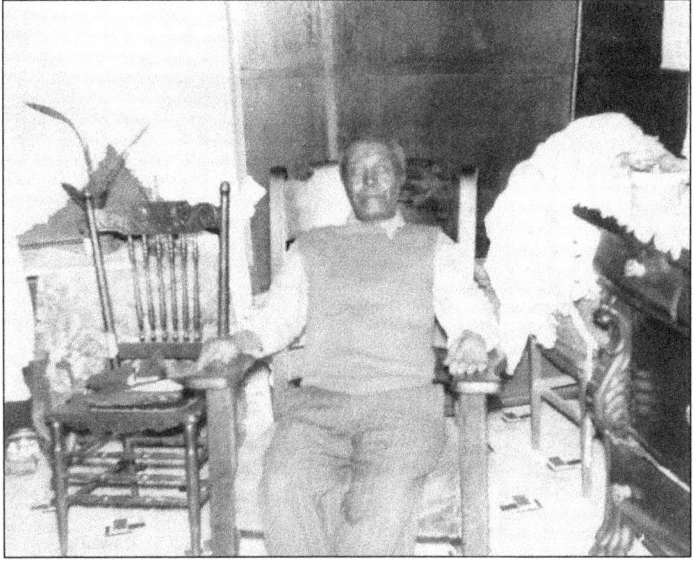

Fred Boling was one of the sons of Eli Boling who lived in a small house on the south side of Aloe Street near New Orleans Avenue. Fred died in 1974 at the age of 98. He served in the infantry during World War I, and because he spoke fluent German, received the nickname "Fritzi."

A 1953 snowstorm finds George W. Otto in front of his neighbor William Townsend's house with the author and his friend Rudy Rundio on the left. Photographer, newspaper editor, artist, and musician, Otto lived at 103 Washington Avenue. In the background stands Einseidel's kiln building on the left and Beyer's automobile agency on the right.

This August 1938 photograph shows city postmistress Mamie Stone and Charles Edison (center) at the Atlantic County Agricultural Fair. The Agriculture Fair president Henry Tapken (with hat in hand) and his wife, Anna, are on the left. Edison was elected governor of New Jersey in 1940. The final year of the fair was 1941, when the fair was opened by Vice Pres. Henry Wallace.

Jean Henderson Weigand was one of the first classes of enlisted Women Marines at Hunter College in the Bronx, New York. Her primary duty was as a recruiter. Her final assignment was at the Office of the Joint Chiefs of Staff in Washington, D.C., where one of her last wartime duties was to serve as typist of the Japanese Instruments of Surrender.

When Leon Polinski graduated from Egg
Harbor City High School, he was reported
to be the smallest high school graduate in
the United States. Coming in at only 39
inches tall and 46 pounds, he had developed
a strong personality that propelled him
into his many endeavors. Billed as the
"Little Prince," Polinski's timing could not
have been better: he headed to Hollywood
to become a munchkin in *The Wizard of
Oz*. Polinski was also an athlete, doing
national tours as a midget boxer. Television
gave him additional outlets to be on his
own as one of the Johnnies for Philip
Morris cigarettes and as the Oscar Mayer
Weinermobile chef. In his last years, Leon
returned home to be a mini-train engineer
at a nearby children's theme park.

This publicity photograph for the 20th Century Fox western *The Silver Whip* shows Kathleen Crowley with actor Dale Robertson. She also appeared on the small screen in *Waterfront* with Preston Foster, *Gunsmoke* with James Arness, and *Rockford Files* with James Garner.

Possibly the most famous resident Egg Harbor City has ever produced was "Peace Pilgrim." Born Mildred Norman in 1908, "Peace Pilgrim" decided to devote her life to a pilgrimage for peace. Her message was that if everyone developed inner peace then there would be no need for conflict. From 1953 to 1981, she walked across the United States, more than 25,000 miles, without money and owning only her clothes, a comb, and a toothbrush. She believed that all would be provided, be it food, lodging, etc., and it was. (www.peacepilgrim.org.)

You have come to the end of this travel into the history of Egg Harbor City, brought to you by the Egg Harbor City Historical Society, the Roundhouse Museum, and their supporters. You have seen a fraction of the images and historical information available to the visitors of the museum. Just two months before this book went to the editor, the museum was given a part of history in memory of Police Chief Philip Reinhard by his family. Seen next to the museum is the traffic light control box that for many years sat on the southeast corner of Philadelphia Avenue at US-30. Within the "box" is the original three-color vertical light that is seen in several of the preceding photographs. It now joins the 1905 Lincoln Park fountain and an H. W. Breder Livery hitching post outside the museum.

Visit us at
arcadiapublishing.com

www.ingramcontent.com/pod-product-compliance
Lightning Source LLC
Chambersburg PA
CBHW080625110426
42813CB00006B/1606